Christ and Antichrist

PROCEEDINGS of the
MORMON THEOLOGY SEMINAR

The PROCEEDINGS OF THE MORMON THEOLOGY SEMINAR series is based on a novel idea: that Mormons do theology. Doing theology is different from weighing history or deciding doctrine. Theology speculates. It experiments with questions and advances hypotheses. It tests new angles and pulls loose threads.

The Mormon Theology Seminar organizes interdisciplinary, collaborative, theological readings of Latter-day Saint scripture. Seminar participants with diverse backgrounds closely explore familiar texts in creative ways. In partnership with the Laura F. Willes Center for Book of Mormon Studies at the Neal A. Maxwell Institute for Religious Scholarship, the Mormon Theology Seminar presents these experiments upon the word to foster greater theological engagement with basic Mormon texts.

Series Editor
Brian M. Hauglid

Other MORMON THEOLOGY SEMINAR *books include:*

Adam S. Miller, ed.,
An Experiment on the Word: Reading Alma 32

Joseph M. Spencer and Jenny Webb, eds.,
Reading Nephi Reading Isaiah: 2 Nephi 26–27

Julie M. Smith, ed.,
Apocalypse: Reading Revelation 21–22

Jeremiah John and Joseph M. Spencer, eds.,
Embracing the Law: Reading Doctrine and Covenants 42

Adam S. Miller, ed.,
Fleeing the Garden: Reading Genesis 2–3

Adam S. Miller, ed.,
A Dream, a Rock, and a Pillar of Fire: Reading 1 Nephi 1

mi.byu.edu/pmts

Christ and Antichrist

Reading Jacob 7

Edited by
Adam S. Miller
Joseph M. Spencer

NEAL A. MAXWELL
INSTITUTE *for*
RELIGIOUS SCHOLARSHIP

Brigham Young University
Provo, Utah

A Proceedings of the Mormon Theology Seminar book

Neal A. Maxwell Institute, Provo 84602 | maxwellinstitute.byu.edu

Library of Congress Cataloging-in-Publication Data

Names: Mormon Theology Seminar (2015 : New York, N.Y.), author. | Miller, Adam S., editor. | Spencer, Joseph M., editor. | Mormon Theology Seminar. Proceedings of the Mormon Theology Seminar.
Title: Christ and Antichrist : reading Jacob 7 / edited by Adam S. Miller, Joseph M. Spencer.
Description: Provo, Utah : Neal A. Maxwell Institute, Brigham Young University, [2017] | Series: Proceedings of the Mormon Theology Seminar
Identifiers: LCCN 2017036211| ISBN 9780842530040 (print : alk. paper) | ISBN 9780842530064 (kindle)
Subjects: LCSH: Book of Mormon. Jacob—Congresses. | Church of Jesus Christ of Latter-day Saints—Doctrines—Congresses. | Mormon Church—Doctrines—Congresses.
Classification: LCC BX8627 .M6723 2015 | DDC 289.3/22—dc23
LC record available at https://lccn.loc.gov/2017036211

∞ This paper meets the requirements of ANSI/NISO z39.48-1992 (Permanence of Paper).

ISBN 978-0-8425-3004-0

Cover and book design: Jenny Webb and Andrew Heiss

Printed in the United States of America

Contents

Acknowledgments

Our thanks to the Laura F. Willes Center for Book of Mormon Studies and the Neal A. Maxwell Institute for Religious Scholarship for their generous support of the Mormon Theology Seminar. Without their support, the live, two-week format for the seminar would not be possible. More, a special thanks to Union Theological Seminary in New York City and Dean Mary C. Boys for their willingness to host this Mormon Theology Seminar on Jacob 7.

Introduction

THE BOOK OF MORMON PRESENTS ITSELF AS THE WORK, principally, of three men. The book is of course named after its chief architect, Mormon, a military captain and prophet-historian who witnessed the collapse of a thousand-year-old civilization. Mormon saw the need to tell his people's story in a sweeping one-volume narrative, brilliant but tortured in its execution. But as he came to the end of his literary efforts, he apparently felt that his book remained incomplete, and so he left the record to his son Moroni to finish off. Moroni at first seems to have felt content just to supplement his father's book with a brief epilogue, but he eventually found himself driven to add substantially to the volume. The Book of Mormon is thus, in its final form, as much the work of Moroni as of Mormon. Although the book takes its name from Mormon, it was Moroni who brought the book to the attention of Joseph Smith and who is said to hold the keys over the record.

Because of a complicated series of events, however, readers of the Book of Mormon encounter another major voice long before they become acquainted with either Mormon or Moroni. The volume opens with the lengthy record of Nephi, writings originally assembled some nine or ten centuries before Mormon and Moroni began their work on the book. And thanks to his larger-than-life presence, Nephi has become, in Mormon culture, the book's most recognizable hero. His story is interesting and inspiring, and his prophecies are the most compelling in the whole book. Although Mormon's inclusion of Nephi's writings in the Book of Mormon was ultimately the result of an afterthought, Nephi clearly joins Mormon and Moroni as a major contributor to the project. Mormon's discovery of Nephi's writings seems to have altered the direction of his own project, and there is substantial evidence that Moroni became especially familiar with Nephi's writings.

Though the distinct but intertwined projects of Nephi, Mormon, and Moroni are undeniably rich, it is too easy to allow them to crowd out another important contributor to the Book of Mormon. Far too little attention has been given to the prophet Jacob, Nephi's younger brother, and his importance to the Book of Mormon as a project has consequently often been overlooked.

Jacob was arguably the first great Nephite theologian. It was to him that his father, Lehi, directed what readers encounter as the first substantive treatment of grand theological themes (see 2 Nephi 2), and it was Jacob who first developed those themes in what remains one of the richest chapters in the whole of the Book of Mormon (see 2 Nephi 9). Jacob's teachings on atonement and grace clearly influenced Nephi's thinking (compare 2 Nephi 10:23–25 and 2 Nephi 25:23), just as they influenced much later Book of Mormon prophets like Benjamin, Abinadi, and Alma and Amulek (see Mosiah 3; 15–16; Alma 12; 34; 42). Jacob's careful work on the interpretation of Isaiah also deeply informed Nephi's understanding of that prophet (compare 1 Nephi 22 with 2 Nephi 25, mediated by 2 Nephi 6 and 10), and he quite uniquely gave detailed attention to a prophet the Book of Mormon presents as having been an influence on Isaiah himself (see Jacob 4–6). Jacob was the first Nephite prophet to defend cultural minorities (see Jacob 2–3), and his willingness to speak truth to power provided a model for some of the most important prophetic interventions in later Lehite history (see especially Mosiah 11–12 and Helaman 13–16). Further, Jacob's confrontation with an enemy of Nephite Christian religion (see Jacob 7) set the tone for similar confrontations later in Nephite history (see Alma 1 and 30). Although the book that bears his name is rather short, comparatively, Jacob's imprint on the Book of Mormon is impressive.

With these considerations in mind, the second annual summer seminar in Mormon theology, cosponsored by the Mormon Theology

Seminar and the Neal A. Maxwell Institute for Religious Scholarship and generously funded by the Laura F. Willes Center for Book of Mormon Studies, convened in 2015 in New York City to study the seventh and final chapter of the book of Jacob. Graciously hosted for two weeks by Union Theological Seminary, eight scholars from a variety of disciplines and with a variety of interests sat down to read, with great care and a great many questions, the story of Jacob's confrontation with Sherem, the notorious critic of Christianity. We hoped to learn from the story itself, as well as from theological statements embedded in the narrative. We also hoped to see how the story relates itself literarily to other stories in Mormon scripture, as well as to understand the philosophical implications of the rival conceptions of law and the messianic on display in the text. And of course, we hoped to experience the sense of camaraderie that attends collaborative reading of a sacred text.

It is impossible to reproduce in writing the depth and richness of the seminar as an experience. Mornings were dedicated to individual preparation for our collaborative work, with each participant producing notes and a short essay on just a few verses of Jacob 7. Early each afternoon, we met as a group to discuss the text and to share our essays with one another. We spent between four and six hours each afternoon working together on the details of the scriptural text—trying to understand the determinations and the ambiguities of the narrative, teasing out the theological and philosophical presuppositions of the text, and raising many more questions than we could possibly hope to answer. After just a few days, however, a set of identifiable questions emerged as central to our collaborative reading, and our several interests in the text began to take clearer shape. As our first week of work came to an end, we began to turn our attention from working directly on the text to formulating both our shared and our private conclusions. The papers that make up this volume were written, in their first form, over the course of our second week together. We worked on each other's ideas, listened to each other's papers, and tried to organize our thoughts about the questions that had come to interest us all. And at the end of the second week, we hosted a public symposium to present our preliminary conclusions.

This volume collects our conclusions in a somewhat more finalized form than that in which they were presented in New York. It opens with a summary of our findings, written collaboratively and meant to outline a few of the things we came to focus on over the course of our work together. The summary report presents these findings in the form of complex answers to apparently straightforward questions. Nonetheless, the conclusions drawn in these summary findings are anything but conclusive. They summarize our discussions and our shared interests, but they don't come even close to exhausting the virtuosity of the text. If there's anything to be learned from sitting down for two weeks to read a chapter of the Book of Mormon together, it's that at least a year of such work would be needed to feel like the basic implications of the text have been decently addressed. The conclusions shared in the summary report, then, are merely provisional, meant more to serve as an invitation than to decide on the meaning of the text. We hope others will see these points of possible interpretation as a spur to provide better and closer readings, richer and more poignant readings. Indeed we hope that each of these seminars—this is one of many—helps just to begin a longer conversation about the richness of Mormon scripture.

Of course, once the seminar had come to a conclusion, each of its participants had time to develop her or his own private interests in Jacob 7 somewhat further. This is what makes up the bulk of this volume—more mature versions of the papers presented at the conclusion of the seminar in 2015. In the chapters that follow, then, several themes within the story of Jacob's encounter with Sherem find fuller articulation. They deserve some introduction here, if only to prepare the reader to appreciate them better.

The book opens with Jana Riess's "'There Came a Man': Sherem, Scapegoating, and the Inversion of Prophetic Tradition." Riess discusses the importance of the formulaic opening words of Jacob's story—"and there came a man among the people"—which ironically borrows a trope from stories of prophetic intervention in the Hebrew Bible. In scripture, the formula almost universally introduces a story about a nameless "man of God" who appears from nowhere to deliver an uncomfortable message to those in power, usually with rather drastic consequences. In Jacob 7, oddly, the formula introduces Sherem, the man who demands a sign rather than delivers one. To develop this reversal of expectations, Riess draws on the literary and anthropological theory of René Girard, exploring the uncomfortable outcome of Sherem's intervention. Sherem is struck dead, but in such a way that Nephite society turns its collective attention in a new and perhaps unprecedented way to their responsibility for (as well as their antipathy toward) the estranged Lamanites, their brothers and sisters.

Riess's study asks readers to confront deep ambiguities in Jacob 7, including the possibility that a deeply inspired and inspiring narrative bears within it ethically troubling details. Adam Miller, in "Reading Signs or Repeating Symptoms," further explores suggestions in the text of the Sherem story that its moral lessons are fraught and ambiguous. On Miller's reading, Jacob tells a story that's at once triumphalistic and tragic. The prophet triumphs over true doctrine's foe, yet the prophet clearly mispredicts the behavior of that foe. Jacob tells Sherem he would deny any sign granted because of the devil's influence, but Sherem, after seeing a sign, genuinely seeks repentance and helps launch a large-scale Nephite return to true religion. Jacob has apparently fallen into the trap of viewing Sherem through a lens colored by his difficult experiences with his older brothers, brothers who were, like Sherem, committed to the Mosaic regime and unsure about Nephi and Jacob and their "doctrine of Christ." Beautifully, however, Miller notes that the story ends with Jacob's surprise at the turn of events—and with his leading his people in a new attempt to reach out to the children of his older brothers.

Kim Berkey also finds in Jacob 7 a story of development and maturation. In "The Lord's Prayer(s) in Jacob 7," she looks carefully at the way the most dramatic parts of the Sherem story—his being struck down, his subsequent confession, and his eventual spectacular death—are organized around two prayers offered by Jacob. Further, Berkey shows, each of the two prayers contains within it an allusion to important prayers spoken by Jesus Christ in the New Testament's Synoptic Gospels: the Lord's Prayer from the Sermon on the Mount and Christ's desperate prayer in the Garden of Gethsemane. Strikingly, the earlier of Jacob's two prayers, uttered in close connection with his misprediction of Sherem's response to the divinely granted sign, finds him struggling to reconcile his will to God's, while the later of the two prayers, offered after Jacob has watched events turn in a new direction, shows him simply requesting something of his Father in Heaven and seeing it granted. In the place of a kind of tortured asceticism, in imitation of Christ's suffering in the garden, Jacob's more mature prayer exhibits a deep intimacy with God that simply follows the prayer the Lord recommends to his followers in his most famous sermon. The larger story of Jacob 7 can thus be read, Berkey argues, as outlining a theology of right and proper prayer.

Jacob Rennaker's "Divine Dream Time: The Hope and Hazard of Revelation" argues that a theology of time accompanies any theology of prayer on offer in Jacob 7. Rennaker takes his cue, interestingly, from Jacob's famously melancholy farewell, included only after the Sherem story has come to its conclusion. For Rennaker, Jacob's talk of the dreamlike passage of time provides a useful metaphor for Jacob's messianic experience of time. Sherem's defense of the law of Moses is rooted in a linear conception of time, uninterruptable by any messianic surprise. Jacob, on the other hand, lives a life of hope that draws the future into the present, interrupting the smooth flow of time, causing him to experience time in a fundamentally distinct way. The hazard of revelation thus lies in the tortured sense of time that accompanies it, and Rennaker goes so far as to suggest that Sherem's being struck might well have been a direct consequence of his being granted, for a moment at least, a glimpse into messianic time. Unable to reorient the present to a messianic future, Sherem collapses in fear. By contrast, Jacob continues his ministry in hope.

Similarly invested in questions of time and hope is Jeremy Walker's paper, "'To Destroy Us Continually': Time and the *Katechon* in Jacob 7." Walker addresses himself to the peculiar phrase Jacob uses to describe ongoing Nephite conflict with Lamanites, the latter attempting to "destroy [the Nephites] continually." Taking the ambiguities of this phrase as a point of departure—it might refer to continued attempts to destroy the Nephites, but the wording also suggests a paradoxical act of continually destroying someone or something—Walker looks at a whole series of problems associated with time in Jacob. After a substantial summary of theoretical resources (drawn primarily from the philosopher Giorgio Agamben), the essay narrows in particularly on an idea Walker calls "messianic oscillation." Faithful anticipation of the Messiah's arrival (in Jarom's wording: "as though he already was") makes the time of faith a harrowing experience, a time oscillating between hopefulness and hopelessness as it interweaves present and future. All this Walker puts in dialogue with a notion drawn from Paul's second letter to the Thessalonians: the *katechon*, a force that restrains the forces of evil but simultaneously postpones the anticipated arrival of the Messiah. Jacob beautifully expresses the tensions inherent in every attempt at resisting evil in his concluding farewell, where hope and despair seem to alternate in quick succession.

Joseph Spencer's contribution to the volume also takes its orientation from Jacob's concluding farewell. But where Rennaker and Walker place the farewell within larger questions about temporality, Spencer's "Weeping for Zion" gives detailed attention just to the farewell itself, largely setting the Sherem story aside in order to ask what might be learned from Jacob's melancholy words. Spencer shows that the structure of Jacob's farewell focuses the Nephite experience in a peculiar way on the inaccessibility of their lost homeland, the land of Jerusalem. Drawing on psychology and philosophy to distinguish between distressingly pathological and spiritually productive forms of sadness, he argues that Jacob's farewell can be interpreted as modeling the latter. Because what Jacob's people mourned was Jerusalem's loss, his poignant farewell brings into focus his clear interest throughout his sermons and writings in Israel's covenantal destiny. Jacob's tragic tenor, on Spencer's account, exhibits itself in its most concentrated form in the prophet's consecrated weeping for Zion.

Sharon Harris's "Covenant Obligation to Scripture as Covenant Obligation to Family" focuses, like Spencer does, on the way Jacob's story helps to frame the Abrahamic covenant that's so central to Mormonism. Tracing priestly and temple themes that organize the narrative of the Sherem encounter, Harris asks about the importance of the fact that the story culminates in a renewed emphasis on scripture. She notes that the closure of Jacob's book is followed in the Book of Mormon by Enos's report of the sacred event during which Jacob gave him charge of the scriptural record. The transmission of the record is passed within the family, from generation to generation, with language deeply suggestive of covenant. These are significant details in such close connection with a story that's primarily about how to read scripture—whether it is or isn't appropriate to read the canonical law of Moses as messianic in nature. On Harris's reading, Jacob inherits a tradition but must for that very reason reauthor the meaning of the covenant that obligates him. The difficulties attending Jacob's encounter with Sherem thus help to outline the complex nature of covenantal inheritance.

Like Harris, Jenny Webb gives her attention to the role played in Jacob 7 by family and covenant. In "Formed by Family: Jacob 7 as a Site for Sealing," however, Webb roots her reading in the easily overlooked theme of flesh and family that often draws Jacob's attention in his preaching and writing. Reviewing in great detail Jacob's most intimate relations, Webb helps to reveal how all of Jacob's family are implicitly woven into the story of the prophet's encounter with Sherem. Distressingly, Jacob's experience with Sherem takes place long after Jacob's loved ones have disappeared or been estranged, adding poignancy to his self-understanding as a wanderer at odds with his errant brothers and cousins. Yet in a way, they all live again in his present experience. And importantly, Webb argues that Jacob's experience with Sherem finds echoes in the record of the child of his own flesh, Enos. Jacob 7 thus becomes the heart of a larger network of family relations, binding together the people Jacob could not keep close to him in life.

Jacob 7 is an excessively rich text. These papers only scratch the surface. We hope that readers of this volume can glimpse some of that same depth as they work through our reflections and begin to formulate some of their own.

—Joseph M. Spencer

Summary Report

Question 1: Who is Sherem?

JACOB INTRODUCES SHEREM AS SOMEONE who does not belong. "There came a man among the people of Nephi," Jacob tell us, "whose name was Sherem." Describing Sherem as someone who "came among" the Nephites, Jacob implies that Sherem was not, in some sense, already among them (Jacob 7:1).[1] It seems unlikely, though, that Sherem is an outsider in any culturally or ethnically substantial way. Sherem arrives fully informed about Jacob, the law of Moses, and the doctrine of Christ, and he arrives with a clearly defined mission in relation to all three. More, Sherem arrives on the scene with "a perfect knowledge of the language of the people," something unlikely for a foreigner (v. 4). Either way, the rhetorical force of Jacob's implication is to position Sherem antagonistically as "not one of us." Given the difficulties faced by Jacob himself as a preacher (see Jacob 1–3), his wariness regarding his rival is expected and understandable.

Jacob also reports that Sherem was a preacher, that he did not accept the "doctrine of Christ," that he had a perfect knowledge of the

---

1. Throughout this volume, we have used Royal Skousen's *The Book of Mormon: The Earliest Text* (New Haven: Yale University Press, 2009) for our base text, providing a note wherever we have used another edition.

language of the people, that he spoke persuasively, that he quickly gathered a following, and that he labored diligently (Jacob 7:2–4). In short,
Sherem is a popular, hardworking, talented, and eloquent preacher who
is committed to defending the law of Moses. Jacob immediately frames
Sherem's missionary efforts in terms of "flattery," "lead[ing] away the
hearts of the people," and "the power of the devil" (vv. 3–4). However,
unlike others in the Book of Mormon who oppose the doctrine of
Christ, Sherem explicitly does so in defense of the law of Moses, what he
calls "the right way of God" (v. 7). Backed by key Mosaic prohibitions,
Sherem defends God and charges Jacob with the crimes of blasphemy
(misappropriating God's name and law) and divination (claiming to
tell the future). In light of these elements, together with the story's
rhetorical dynamics, it is plausible to read Sherem as a preacher who is
well-meaning but wrong, rather than someone who is evil.

Sherem, arguing against the doctrine of Christ and in defense of
the law of Moses, would surely have reminded Jacob of similar argu-
ments made by those in Jerusalem against Lehi's messianic prophecies
and by Laman and Lemuel against Nephi's own prophecies (cf. 1 Nephi
17:22). Throughout their encounter, Jacob automatically assumes, as
Nephi did with Laman or Lemuel, that Sherem acts in bad faith and
with the worst possible motives. Rather than offering instruction or
correction (at least as he tells the story), Jacob moves immediately to
condemnation. And, most tellingly, Jacob is convinced that, even if
Sherem were given a sign from God, Sherem would doubtless deny
that sign and refuse to repent (Jacob 7:14). But, it turns out, Jacob is
wrong on this last point. When the sign is given and Sherem is smitten,
Sherem not only repents but immediately "confesse[s] the Christ and
the power of the Holy Ghost" (v. 17). It is thus Sherem's preaching—not
Jacob's—that the multitude ultimately witnesses, that astonishes them,
and that calls down the power of God such that they, too, are overcome
and fall to the earth (v. 21). It is Sherem's preaching rather than Jacob's
that inaugurates a fundamental transformation among the Nephites,
with the result that "the love of God was restored again among the
people" (v. 23).

For his own part, Sherem fears that he has "lied unto God" because
he "denied the Christ and said that [he] believed the scriptures" (Jacob

7:19), but in context this confession reads more like a retroactive acknowledgment of his failure to understand the scriptures than an admission of a malicious intent to deceive the people from the beginning. Of course, Jacob's strident and unyielding evaluation of Sherem as a "wicked man" (v. 23) should not simply be discounted. Certainly Sherem failed to understand the practical and theological importance of Nephite messianic prophecy. But the significant differences between Jacob's evaluation of Sherem and Sherem's own stated goals and morally significant actions, together with the obvious dynamics that may have unfairly colored Jacob's own judgments, indicate that readers should seriously consider reassessing Sherem's words and actions in a more charitable light. The important limitations to his religious outlook can be instructive without vilifying him, and details in the narrative suggest that charity is called for.

Question 2: Where is Jacob?

Sherem dominates the narrative in Jacob 7. Where Sherem is an active, driving presence, Jacob is, curiously and suggestively, passive and peripheral. Note that it is Sherem who comes among the people, Sherem who preaches and labors diligently, and Sherem who has to seek out Jacob for an opportunity to confront him. "He sought much opportunity that he might come unto me," Jacob reports (Jacob 7:3). Why is this necessary? Where is Jacob? Why is he so hard to find? Why does Sherem have to seek much in order to come unto him—especially in such a young society that would likely have been relatively small and intimate at this point? Moreover, why is Sherem allowed time and freedom to "lead away many hearts" without any resistance from Jacob (v. 3)? Why doesn't Jacob take action, seek out Sherem, confront him, and himself put a stop to Sherem's efforts to "overthrow the doctrine of Christ" (v. 2) long before he has sustained success?

In Jacob's telling, Sherem ironically plays the traditionally prophetic part, signaled by the use of the formula "there came a man" at the outset of the narrative (Jacob 7:1). (This formula is most often used in scripture to describe a prophet figure who arrives with an unwelcome message.) Sherem comes among Jacob's people as a prophetic rebel, preaching and organizing, moving the populace to remember the law of Moses, calling them to repentance, and confronting those in power with charges of blasphemy. Jacob oddly plays the part normally assigned in such stories about prophets to a leader like King David or King Noah, while Sherem gets to play the part of a prophet like Nathan or Abinadi, delivering hard truths to a figure of established power. In this way, the typical prophet-priest power dynamic is, at least at the outset of the Sherem narrative, neatly reversed.

It is possible that Jacob's age and institutional power play a more practical part in isolating him from Sherem. Is Jacob too old to take to the streets? Has he withdrawn from his people in light of previous failures (cf. Jacob 1–3)? Has he withdrawn because of his "overanxiety" for his people as a result of their failure to understand the "mystery" that is the doctrine of Christ (Jacob 4:18)? Might he, in his role as a priest in the Nephite temple, effectively live behind the temple walls, insulated from the daily business of his people (cf. Jacob 1:17–19)?

Whatever answers might be given to these questions, even when Jacob does arrive on the scene for his decisive confrontation with Sherem, he is passive. Sherem seeks him out and speaks first, leveling the charge of blasphemy. Jacob counters with a series of questions, but Sherem is the one who actively solicits the sign that ends up smiting him. Jacob somewhat passively gives his blessing to whatever God wills. Sherem is felled by "the power of the Lord" for "the space of many days," and it is Sherem's sincere repentance and preaching that spark the mass conversion that returns the people to the scriptures and their love of God (Jacob 7:15–23). Jacob figures into this decisive conversion that reboots Nephite society as a whole primarily by way of his belated comment that all this happened because he had, earlier and offstage, "requested it of my Father which was in heaven, for he had heard my cry and answered my prayer" (v. 22).

Further, verse 24 then recounts, in the passive voice, that "means were devised" to reclaim the Lamanites, perhaps spearheaded by Jacob, but these efforts "all were vain" (Jacob 7:24). The chapter then concludes with Jacob's melancholic reflections on his old age, suffering, and mourning, all framed by a sense of life passing "away like as it were unto us a dream" (v. 26).

The overall effect of these themes is striking: Jacob's explicit commentary on the narrative action (he is the good prophet and Sherem is the wicked man) is consistently in tension with the narrative actions themselves and, in particular, with Jacob's own framing of that narrative action. Jacob presents himself as passive and peripheral, as both being and not being the hero of his story. This ambiguity, perhaps intentional, may itself be of central theological importance.

Question 3: What, in Jacob 7, is the "doctrine of Christ"?

Concluding his record, Jacob reports that the "lives [of his people] passed away like as it were unto us a dream, we being a lonesome and a solemn people, wanderers cast out from Jerusalem, born in tribulation in a wild wilderness, and hated of our brethren, which caused wars and contentions; wherefore we did mourn out our days" (Jacob 7:26). Jacob mourns because he and his people have lost Jerusalem and, having lost the holy city, they are lonesome and hated by their brethren. Jerusalem is, for Jacob, a focal point. Jacob and his people had lost Jerusalem for the same reason they were hated by his brothers Laman and Lemuel. As Laman and Lemuel put it: "And we know that the people which were in the land of Jerusalem were a righteous people, for they keep the statutes and the judgments of the Lord and all his commandments according to the law of Moses; wherefore we know that they are a righteous people. And our father hath judged them and hath led us away because we would hearken unto his word" (1 Nephi 17:22).

Laman and Lemuel align Jerusalem with the law of Moses, but they find themselves lost in the wilderness because, rather than keeping the law of Moses, they heeded the words of their father, "a visionary man" (1 Nephi 5:4). Being a visionary man, Lehi dreamed dreams. Without these dreams, he would not have "seen the things of God in a vision" or "known the goodness of God," but he would have "tarried at Jerusalem" and "perished with [his] brethren" (1 Nephi 5:4). This visionary intrusion of dreams into everyday life is the fault line that organizes the whole of Book of Mormon history and, ultimately, distinguishes the law of Moses from the doctrine of Christ.

This same drama—this argument about the law of Moses and the doctrine of Christ that Lehi plays out with Jerusalem and Nephi plays out with Laman and Lemuel—is repeated again in Jacob 7 with Sherem and Jacob. Sherem defends the law of Moses and takes Jacob's visionary assimilation of that law to be a perversion of the law's purity. Echoing Laman and Lemuel, Sherem claims that Jacob has "led away much of this people, that they pervert the right way of God and keep not the law of Moses, which is the right way, and convert the law of Moses into the worship of a being which ye say shall come many hundred years hence" (v. 7). For Jacob, however, the right way of God is not grounded directly in the law itself but in visions and revelations, and apparently in a rather specific sort of visions and revelations. He claims that his hope in Christ could not be shaken because of his "many revelations": "For I had truly seen angels and they had ministered unto me. And also I had heard the voice of the Lord speaking unto me in very word from time to time" (v. 5). This revelatory power that cannot be confined within the bounds of the law is, as Jacob says, "the power of the Holy Ghost" (v. 12).

Additionally, this phrase, "the power of the Holy Ghost," is used consistently in Nephi's writings in connection with his visions of the larger history of Israel, God's covenant people. Nephi promises that anyone can gain access to apocalyptic visions of that history (see 1 Nephi 10:17–22). As with Jacob's talk of "the doctrine of Christ" (Jacob 7:2; cf. 2 Nephi 31), his references to the power of the Holy Ghost seem to be part of a larger prophetic heritage passed on to Lehi's children.

Significantly, the basic point of contention in each case is time. According to Sherem, Jacob perverts the law by using his messianic visions to break the time frame and, thus, to pervert the orderly, temporally normative operation of the law. He "pervert[s] the right way of God" and "convert[s] the law of Moses into the worship of a being which ye say shall come many hundred years hence" (Jacob 7:7). This visionary subordination of the law to a promised messiah is "blasphemy, for no man knoweth of such things; for he cannot tell of things to come" (v. 7). Jacob's visions are, in effect, destroying or killing the orderly succession of cause and effect imposed by the law with their present-tense enactment of future-tense events.

On this score Sherem is, in part, correct: the law *is* dying. Nephi and Jacob both advocate a doctrine of Christ that reorders time by treating the law as if it were already fulfilled in Christ. As Nephi puts it: "And notwithstanding we believe in Christ, we keep the law of Moses and look forward with steadfastness unto Christ until the law shall be fulfilled, for for this end was the law given. Wherefore the law hath become dead unto us, and we are made alive in Christ because of our faith, yet we keep the law because of the commandments" (2 Nephi 25:24–25). By converting the law into a machine for reordering time—for treating the past as forgivable, the present as open for action, and the future as already accomplished—the law becomes dead to them and eternal life becomes possible.

Sherem experiences this kind of abrupt temporal reeducation personally when, smitten by "the power of the Lord," he lies comatose for many days (Jacob 7:15). Asleep to the world, he is exposed to eternity: "he spake of hell and of eternity and of eternal punishment" and he "confessed the Christ and the power of the Holy Ghost" (vv. 18, 17). The doctrine of Christ, perhaps initially to our terror, superimposes eternity onto time—that is, it superimposes Christ onto the law—and allows life and law to be seen and lived from the far side of their own completion in Christ. And then, in this visionary space of superimposition, it is only natural that our lives should pass away as in a dream.

Question 4: How does Jacob 7 fit into the larger structure of the book of Jacob?

The book of Jacob is Jacob's unique contribution to the Nephite record. (However, it should be noted that a substantial and significant sermon delivered by Jacob is also included by Nephi in his own record in 2 Nephi 6–10.) Contemporary versions of the book of Jacob break the text into seven chapters. However, the earliest version of the text breaks it more cleanly along thematic lines into just four chapters: Jacob 1, Jacob 2–3, Jacob 4–6, and Jacob 7. Jacob 1 functions as a kind of preface to the book, introducing key themes and providing historical context. Jacob 2–3 records a sermon delivered by Jacob to the Nephites at the time of Nephi's death. Jacob 4–6 introduces, delivers, and then comments on Zenos's world-historical allegory of the olive tree. Jacob 7 concludes the book with Jacob's confrontation with Sherem regarding the doctrine of Christ.

Jacob 7 itself segments into three parts: Jacob 7:1–23 narrates Jacob's confrontation with Sherem; Jacob 7:24–25 recounts a failed attempt to "reclaim and restore the Lamanites to the knowledge of the truth"; and Jacob 7:26–27 concludes the record with some general reflections on the Nephites' condition as a people, while Jacob formally charges his son Enos with care of the small plates.

One noteworthy feature of the book of Jacob's overall structure is that Jacob 7 appears to be Jacob's third (and finally successful) attempt to end his record. Jacob initially brings his record to a close at the end of chapter 3, at the conclusion of the sermon delivered at the time of Nephi's death. After concluding the sermon proper in Jacob 3:11, Jacob takes a stab at a formal ending for the book in verses 12–14: "These plates are called the plates of Jacob, and they were made by the hand of Nephi. And I make an end of speaking these words" (v. 14).

Chapter 4 then reopens the record with an explanation that, though it is difficult to write many words, Jacob hopes now to preserve for his people some "small degree of knowledge concerning us or concerning their fathers" (Jacob 4:2). In particular, he wants future readers to know "that we knew of Christ, and we had a hope of his glory many hundred years before his coming" (v. 4). Jacob's supplementary attempt to preserve this knowledge in the record suggests that his attempts at teaching the doctrine of Christ to his own people during his own life may have had limited success. Jacob 7:7 indirectly suggests the same. There, Sherem suggests that Jacob has "led away much of this people," implying that Jacob has not managed to lead *all* of the people to embrace the doctrine of Christ. Likewise, these hints raise, in general, the question of the extent to which Lehi's, Nephi's, and Jacob's personal revelations concerning the doctrine of Christ were available to the Nephite people at large. Regardless, Jacob attempts to bring the record to a close a second time in Jacob 6:12–13. Wrapping up his comments on Zenos's allegory, Jacob simply concludes: "O be wise! What can I say more? Finally, I bid you farewell until I shall meet you before the pleasing bar of God, which bar striketh the wicked with awful dread and fear. Amen."[2]

It appears, then, that Jacob intended to firmly conclude his record with Jacob 6 but that, in the years that followed, his encounter with Sherem so moved him as to motivate the addition of one final coda to his brother's plates. Having recounted this confrontation, chapter 7 concludes with a formal charge of transmission, leaving the plates in his son's hands and, directly addressing the reader, offering a final goodbye: "And to the reader I bid farewell, hoping that many of my brethren may read my words. Brethren, adieu" (Jacob 7:27).

Jacob's profoundly melancholy concluding reflection on the Nephites' situation as a people—"our lives passed away like as it were unto us a dream, we being a lonesome and a solemn people, wanderers cast out from Jerusalem, born in tribulation in a wild wilderness, and hated of our brethren, which caused wars and contentions; wherefore we did mourn out our days" (Jacob 7:26)—together with the "anxiety" that he frequently ascribes to himself (cf. 2 Nephi 6:3; Jacob 1:5; 2:3; 4:18), may supply some crucial context for his apparent inability to cleanly bring his record to a close. Finally, insofar as melancholy and anxiety are potentially significant affects with respect to a life lived in Christ, the tripartite stop-and-go structure of Jacob's book may itself be of theological significance.

Further, in its final form, the book of Jacob ends with an unmistakable turn for the better. After Jacob's apparent inability to sway the whole of his people toward righteousness after Nephi's death (see Jacob 1–3), he seems to have largely given up hope of seeing his people return, generally, to righteousness. The story of Sherem, in all its complexity, tells the story of at least a temporary refocusing of the Nephites on their religious and spiritual duties. Jacob 7, in its supplemental fashion, allows the book of Jacob to end on a happy note, anticipating the more widely spread Christian following on display in subsequent narratives in the Book of Mormon.

---

2. Skousen, *Book of Mormon*, uses "the *pleading* bar of God" in Jacob 6:13.

"There Came a Man": Sherem, Scapegoating, and the Inversion of Prophetic Tradition

Jana Riess

Sherem appears seemingly out of the blue in Jacob 7:1 ("there came a man"), showing up among the people of Nephi with no indication of his origins. Various commentators have speculated that he was a Nephite, or possibly a wandering Jaredite, Mulekite, or Zoramite.[1] But our attention might be better placed in parsing the deceptively simple phrase "there came a man." This essay explores several places in which this phrase appears in parallel formations in the Hebrew Bible and discusses how its use in Jacob 7 carefully inverts the prophetic tradition established in those biblical texts. Sherem, as will become clear, is not the "man of God" who appears in the Hebrew Bible stories but is something else entirely. To ascertain what that role might be, the second half of the chapter then reflects upon how Sherem's

---

1. For an overview of several different theories, see A. Keith Thompson, "Who Was Sherem?" *Interpreter: A Journal of Mormon Scripture* 14 (2015): 1–15. Thompson rejects the notion that Sherem was a Mulekite or Jaredite largely because there is no evidence of interactions between those people and the Nephites until much later in the Book of Mormon narrative. Thompson says that Sherem's eloquent fluency with the Nephite language and the depth of his knowledge of the law of Moses suggest that it is more likely Sherem was a fellow Nephite from the Zoramite line.

death unites the people against a common enemy, functioning as a classic scapegoat in René Girard's formulation.[2] We will see that the Sherem story is, over and over again, one that consistently reverses well-established expectations.

The *Ish Elohim* in the Hebrew Bible

When we first meet Sherem, we are simply told that "there came a man among the people of Nephi whose name was Sherem" (Jacob 7:1). There are echoes here of six places in the Hebrew Bible where similar language is used and similar situations become apparent. In Hebrew, the phrase "man of God" (*ish elohim*) has special significance as "someone with extraordinary and rather frightening power and insight," who "knows things you might not want him to know and does things you might not want him to do," says biblical scholar John Goldingay.[3] The *ish elohim* is a stand-in for God, speaking with God's voice. Let us analyze three of these passages to identify a general pattern.

First, in 1 Samuel 2:27,[4] we hear that "a man of God came" to the priest Eli to excoriate him about his two shameful sons, who have no interest in the Lord. They have dishonored their father and the Lord by skimming the fat from the top of the sacrifices while the meat is yet raw and by sleeping with loose women at the entrance to the tent of meeting.[5] The mysterious, unnamed man of God tells Eli that the Lord has had just about enough of this; even though Eli and his sons are the direct biological heirs to the priestly line, God has decided to restructure. Eli is going to lose his job, and his sons will both die on the same day.

---

2. I am grateful to Jeremy Walker for first suggesting the connection between Jacob 7 and René Girard's theory of the scapegoat.

3. John Goldingay, *1 and 2 Kings for Everyone* (Louisville, KY: Westminster John Knox Press, 2011), 197.

4. Unless I indicate otherwise, I use the New Revised Standard Version of the Bible for my biblical quotations.

5. Francesca Aran Murphy notes that the phrase "tent of meeting" is an anachronism, which "updates the scenario to the original audience's frame of reference." Murphy, *1 Samuel* (Grand Rapids, MI: Brazos Press, 2010), 24.

In this first story, the man of God inverts the expected line of priestly succession. Eli's sons have all of the right lineage but none of the faithfulness; the story repeatedly contrasts them with Samuel, a young boy who has been given up to the temple by his mother in gratitude for his miraculous conception. The stories are woven together in vignettes, causing Walter Brueggemann to note that "'the rise of Samuel' is narrated in counterpoint to the account of 'Eli's fall'" and that "there is irony in the fact that [Samuel] is nurtured in faith by Eli, the very one whom he displaces."[6] It is to Samuel that the priesthood will pass, not to the abusive sons of Eli. The *ish elohim* has delivered a message of change, showing that God cares less for lineage than for obedience and devotion. Samuel's ascendancy as the new priest signals a larger change as well: it will later be Samuel who inaugurates and blesses an entirely new system of government, choosing Israel's first monarch.[7]

The second story appears in 1 Kings 13:1, when a man of God from Judah comes to King Jeroboam in Bethel to inform him that his worship practices are all wrong; he's not supposed to be erecting altars anywhere he wants to or designating his own priests outside the line of succession. The stranger prophesies that God's punishment to Jeroboam will be that every unqualified upstart whom Jeroboam has ever taken on as a priest will be burned to death on that very altar.[8] But even after all this, the narrator tells us, "Jeroboam did not turn from his evil way" (1 Kings 13:33).

One relevant fact about this story for our purposes is that the *ish elohim* here is clearly a foreigner, a Judahite who presumes to speak to a king in Israel.[9] But another point is something that comes a bit

---

6. Walter Brueggemann, *First and Second Samuel*, Interpretation series (Louisville, KY: John Knox Press, 1990), 22.

7. Brueggemann, *First and Second Samuel*, 24.

8. One of several ironies in the Jeroboam material is that the man of God prophesies that many years hence, false priests will be sacrificed on that very altar, but then the "sign" that accompanies this prophecy is that the altar in question is immediately and completely destroyed.

9. As John Goldingay notes, it's salient to ask why God had to send a prophet from so far away; was there no righteous prophet to be found in the northern kingdom? Goldingay, *1 and 2 Kings for Everyone*, 64.

deeper into the story, when the visiting man of God has delivered his message and unwisely accepts an invitation to dine at the home of someone who introduces himself as a fellow prophet. God has already commanded the *ish elohim* to deliver his message and return straight home; however, the man of God relaxes and accepts the invitation to dinner. He is soon afterward slain by a lion. This is the only example in the Hebrew Bible where the visiting man of God himself is a morally compromised character who disobeys God's commandment, something that will come up again in our discussion of Sherem.

A third story merits mention here. In 1 Kings 20:28, a man of God comes to King Ahab of Israel to bring him the good news that his tiny group of Israelite forces will indeed be able to defeat the huge army that's invading from Syria. But Ahab's favor does not last long. Right after the battle, he spares the life of the opposing king, calling him "my brother" (v. 32). Contemporary readers may approve of this tender act of reconciliation, but Yahweh has other ideas: Ahab's own life is forfeit because he has allowed himself to enter into a covenant with a foreign, pagan king (v. 42). It takes the Lord some time to get around to this particular smiting, however. It isn't until the following chapter that Ahab and his pagan wife, Jezebel, finally test Yahweh's patience to the point of no return when they decide to seize Naboth's vineyard and accuse that innocent man of blasphemy. Moreover, it isn't until 2 Kings 9 that God's final judgment comes upon the couple. But the Lord's punishment, while not swift, is thorough: chapter 10 details the slaughter of all of Ahab and Jezebel's descendants so that no one of their line will remain to take the throne.

All three of these stories pertain to a prophetic, kingly, or priestly U-turn.[10] Such political reversals have to do with wrong worship

---

10. As an aside, it is interesting that so many of these stories share the common theme of evildoers meeting violent ends in the jaws of wild beasts. In 1 Kings 13:24–25, the man of God is killed by a lion after he has accepted the hospitality of a self-proclaimed prophet in the north. In 1 Kings 20:36, a prophet is slain by a lion when he refuses to smite a second prophet who requests it. Later in 1 Kings, Ahab and Jezebel have their blood licked up by wild dogs after their deaths (his in battle, hers from a fall); the text suggests that Jezebel's body was also eaten by the dogs. See Josey Bridges Snyder, "Jezebel and Her Interpreters," in *Women's Bible*

committed by people who inherited their responsibilities and were not directly called by God. Eli's sons have defiled the priesthood they inherited. Jeroboam has set up shrines outside of Jerusalem and defiled the monarchy he inherited. Ahab and Jezebel not only worship false foreign gods but also try to seize someone else's property. Here they deeply misunderstand God's provisions for distributing the promised land—another aspect of inheritance.[11] They have tried to snatch what is not theirs, what God has apportioned to another.[12]

All these stories have to do with God punishing those who dishonor him by false worship or faithless service. They teach that inherited status is not enough; whether you are a king or a priest or a prophet, you have to earn your keep by unwavering devotion.

Commentary: Twentieth Anniversary Edition, Revised and Updated, ed. Carol A. Newsom, Sharon H. Ringe, and Jacqueline E. Lapsley (Louisville, KY: Westminster John Knox Press, 2012), 180–83.

11. See Goldingay, *1 and 2 Kings for Everyone*, 95.

12. In a fourth story, their son Ahaziah seeks physical healing from a prophet of Baal rather than from Elijah and is found out by the man of God, who prophesies that Ahaziah's foxhole conversion to Baal in a time of need will result in the king's imminent death. The text, interestingly enough, does not immediately identify Elijah, who is unnamed by the messengers who initially encounter him on the road (there came "a man to meet us," says 2 Kings 1:6), in keeping with the mysterious *ish elohim* tradition. The fifth story is in 2 Kings 4, in which Elijah's protégé Elisha spends his energies saving widows, resurrecting children, and staving off starvation one miracle at a time. Here the term *ish elohim* is used to reflect the faith of those who seek out his services, like the mother who puts her dead boy on a donkey and rides many miles to find Elisha, who can bring her child back to life. In these stories, no major reversals of power are attendant. The phrase "man of God" does not signal a new priestly or kingly order, though it does presage unexpected reversals of a happier kind: life where there has been no life, stew in the pot that was empty, oil and bread miraculously multiplied to ward off certain death. The sixth and final example is found in 2 Chronicles 25, when King Amaziah casts his lot with the gods of Edom—inexplicably so, for they are the powerless gods of the land he just conquered with Yahweh's help. Amaziah's punishment in this tale reflects a return to the significance of the man of God for the political and the national, not just the personal.

Sherem and the inversion of prophetic tradition

What does this have to do with Sherem?

Sherem's story begins with the very same setup. "There came a man" among the people, teaching and preaching. Like the prophets of the Hebrew Bible, Sherem seeks out someone in a position of power to speak critically about the dangers that can occur when a society is not adhering to Mosaic law. He is hoping to shake up someone in authority (see Jacob 7:5), someone who has fallen away from the strictest practice of the law and the commandments, someone who is interested in a newfangled god from somewhere else—indeed, even from another time entirely. That someone is Jacob, the high priest. Sherem comes into this text as a watchman over public piety, an outsider who is poised to rein in the people of Nephi from what he sees as a dangerous theological heresy. They are straying from the foundation of their religion, which is the law, and adding to it with this foreign god called the Christ.[13]

Sherem, as an upholder of the law, would have been very familiar with what happens whenever Yahweh's covenant people abandon their foundations and begin to show an openness to worshipping anyone but Yahweh, who admits to being a jealous god. Those stories never end well. So Sherem enters this scene as a trope, as the mysterious man of God whose function is to be more priestly than the priest, to save the people from the brink of ritual disaster.

But this is where the similarities end. In some ways, the Sherem story is a reversal of the expected reversal. In most of the Hebrew Bible

---

13. There may be other ways in which the Nephites are not observing Mosaic law to Sherem's satisfaction. Perhaps he is angry that women have been allowed in the temple (see Jacob 2:7), for example. The text does not specify the ways in which the Nephites "pervert the right way of God" (Jacob 7:7); it is enough that Sherem believes they are flirting with serious theological error. Book of Mormon commentator Monte S. Nyman believes that the presence of women suggests that Jacob's sermon was given on the temple grounds rather than in the temple proper. However, the text of Jacob 1:17 simply states that Jacob taught all the people "in the temple," so Nyman's hermeneutic is dubious. This is especially true given Jacob's additional clarification in 2:2 that he came "up into the temple" to preach to the mixed-gender assembly. See Nyman, *These Records Are True: A Teaching Commentary on Jacob through Mosiah* (Orem, UT: Granite, 2003), 18, 21.

stories, the men of God approach people in power, whether temporal or religious, and their very presence signals a changing of the guard. Theological innovation, regarded as idolatry, is quashed. The status quo is upheld in regard to traditional faith but usually reversed in regard to power.

It is important to note that Sherem does not accuse Jacob of being *non*-religious but of being *wrong*-religious. Jacob is forsaking the religion of the past, the one based on Mosaic law, in favor of some unknown, unproven deity that is only reachable via a time machine. When Sherem says there will be no Christ, he has logic and tradition *and religion* on his side. He's also apparently sincere in his belief that Jacob has, like Eli's sons, become a false priest, one who has "perverted" the right way of God. Sherem works hard, laboring diligently (Jacob 7:3); he has a way with people; he is fiercely intelligent; and he is as learned as a person can be when the library of extant literature is so very limited.[14] Jacob as narrator seems to go out of his way to use active verbs that show Sherem's agentive power. Sherem preaches and declares in order to "overthrow" the doctrine of Christ, his intentions always overt and obvious. There is nothing subtle or hidden about Sherem, who is said to have "sought much opportunity" to meet with Jacob and persuade him to embrace his point of view.

Jacob as narrator chooses to reveal a fair amount of information about our interloper. In fact, we know far more about Sherem than we do almost any of the men of God in the Hebrew Bible. With the exceptions of superstars like Elijah and Elisha, all the others go unnamed in those stories. This should be our first of several clues that something is amiss from the usual pattern. Sherem is named from the very first verse that discusses his actions (Jacob 7:1), even though after this chapter he is never mentioned again in the entire Book of Mormon. Jacob *wants* us to know who this stranger is, because to name Sherem is to have power over him. Sherem will not, like the unnamed "men of God" in the prophetic stories, get to serve as God's anonymous messenger,

---

14. See Grant Hardy, *Understanding the Book of Mormon: A Reader's Guide* (New York: Oxford University Press, 2010), 60.

delivering truth and then vanishing in a whiff of mystery. He gets a name, and therefore an infamy.

A second clue is the pointedly missing phrase "of God" in the Old Testament's typical wording that "a man of God" came along. Sherem is not a man of God, even though the story bears many of the external trappings of other man-of-God tales in which a holy outsider speaks truth to power. But Sherem is not speaking truth, and Jacob, as he is wont to hint as his book proceeds and his society degenerates, is not entirely in power. By choosing to craft his story in this way, Jacob is not only highlighting the fact that the strange visitor is a heretic but is also calling attention to his own diminished political and religious position. The people have largely ignored his many warnings about their unrighteous behavior, evidenced by the fact that chapter 7 opens after "some years had passed away" since Jacob has last written and the people don't evince any change until after Sherem's death near the end of the chapter. Jacob's sermonizing has fallen on deaf ears.

Finally, Sherem reveals his own lack of prophetic status in his insistence that God provide a sign to prove what Jacob is teaching is true. In the Hebrew Bible stories, it is the man of God who provides a sign, and the man of God's relationship with Yahweh is so unshakable that he does not even have to ask for it. It simply and dramatically occurs. For example, in 1 Kings 13, the "man of God from Judah" who has decried King Jeroboam's construction of an unauthorized altar provides an immediate and miraculous sign that his judgments are true.

> And he gave a sign the same day, saying, This is the sign
> which the Lord hath spoken; Behold, the altar shall be
> rent, and the ashes that are upon it shall be poured out.
> (1 Kings 13:3, KJV)

The hand with which Jeroboam tries to seize the man of God withers instantly, and the unauthorized altar is torn down in spectacular fashion. By these signs the man of God demonstrates that, as one commentary puts it, "the God who can ensure that prophecy comes to pass in the short term can surely also do so over the longer term."[15] In the Book of Mormon story, by contrast, Sherem reveals that he is not a true "man of God" when he asks Jacob for a sign rather than delivering one himself.

Sherem as scapegoat

We can understand more of this passage by analyzing the social and political roles Sherem and Jacob play, respectively. It is a situation that makes many readers uncomfortable. It feels wrong that Sherem, of all the heretics and shady characters in the Book of Mormon, has to die. Why not Alma the Younger, who persecuted the church so strongly that he sought to destroy it? Alma gets to live while Sherem, who has carefully followed the mandates of Mosaic law, gets struck down. Why? For that matter, why do Jacob's own people, who have been warned repeatedly of their egregious sins over the course of many years, walk away from chapter 7 unscathed while Sherem, who is observant and pious, is dealt a fatal blow after a single episode of outmoded theology? René Girard's theory of the scapegoat may shed light on this dynamic: Sherem has to die because the people need a scapegoat in order to become united and whole, at least for a time.

In Girard's view, something called mimetic desire happens when two people or groups are fighting over the same object. One literature scholar states that an analogy would be two brothers playing on their front porch. One takes a G.I. Joe from the toy box, and then the other makes a grab for it, and a full-on fight ensues. Soon they have forgotten the ostensible reasons they are fighting—exclusive rights to that toy— and are fighting for the sake of fighting. In Girard's view, the fight only stops when an overweight neighbor boy wanders into their yard to see what is going on. "Oh, there's old fat butt!" one brother cries. "Yeah, it's big fat butt!" taunts the other. As the overweight boy runs back to his

---

15. Iain W. Provan, "1 Kings," in *The New Interpreter's Bible One Volume Commentary*, ed. Beverly Roberts Gaventa and David Petersen (Nashville: Abingdon, 2010), 222.

own house crying, the two brothers resume playing with each other, allies once again. Order has been restored.[16]

This disturbing story, according to Girard, occurs over and over again in human interaction. When one person or group claims an object or a privilege, suddenly the other wants it too, imitating the first person's desire. It is called mimetic desire because of this imitative function; if someone else values that thing, the thing itself must be valuable, and therefore we should want it too. The only way to restore order is if a third party functions as a scapegoat to end the conflict. As we will see below, Girard's five necessary steps of scapegoating intersect in interesting ways with the story of Sherem.[17]

Chaos, lack of differentiation, and a blurring of boundaries

We don't know enough about what was going on in Nephite society at the time of Jacob 7 to understand fully how Girard's theory might play out in this passage. However, 2 Nephi and other sections of Jacob reveal that serious tensions existed among the Nephites. Jacob opens this chapter deeply at odds with his own people. Possibly this instability had a political component; Noel Reynolds has noted that although modern readers often assume that the recently deceased Nephi had been the king of the people, there is little evidence within the text to support that idea.[18] If Reynolds is correct about Nephi, this means that Jacob's critique of the ruling Nephite king comes as a further

---

16. Brian McDonald, "Violence and the Lamb Slain: An Interview with Rene Girard," *Touchstone: A Journal of Mere Christianity* (December 2003), http://www.touchstonemag.com/archives/article.php?id=16-10-0-040-8.

17. The helpful typology of these five steps is adapted from "René Girard's Mimetic Desire and *The Scapegoat*," 180Rule (blog), March 31, 2012, accessed online at http://180rule.com/rene-girards-mimetic-theory-the-scapegoat/.

18. Noel B. Reynolds, "Nephite Kingship Reconsidered," in *Mormons, Scripture, and the Ancient World: Studies in Honor of John L. Sorenson*, ed. Davis Bitton (Provo, UT: Foundation for Ancient Research and Mormon Studies, 1998), 151–89. See 2 Nephi 5:18, in which Nephi notes how he rejected the people's desire to set him up as a king, even though he "did for them according to that which was in [his] power."

destabilization: he is not only reproving a sitting monarch, but he is doing so at a time when the regime is new and tenuous. The political situation feels fragile.

Moreover, the Nephites were a people in theological crisis. Recall that Jacob 2 and 3 feature a catalog of all the people's sins—their greed and sexual transgressions and terrible pride. Jacob stands in the temple to deliver his message, one of four "temple sermons" in the Book of Mormon.[19] The scene of his address is no accident. Jacob chooses the holiest and most established place to convict the people of their wrongdoing. The sermon warns of dire eternal consequences that will attend them if they do not harken to Jacob's admonitions, an apocalyptic theme that is picked up again in chapter 6. There everything is coming to a head: they will be destroyed by fire in facing the awful judgment of God. Some form of judgment is mentioned half a dozen times in just this short chapter. And this chaotic situation seems to be the note on which Jacob himself plans to gracefully exit as sacred scribe: he says at the end of chapter 6 that he is making an end of his writing.

Jacob 2, 3, and 6 establish a doomsday scenario in which chaos is encroaching and the people's end may be nigh. The people will be punished for their sins, probably by fire. According to Girard, the fear and trembling engendered by such a situation is precisely the condition in which a scapegoat becomes most necessary. When chaos is looming and danger is real, that is when the people need an expiation.[20]

The other component of Girard's step 1 is a blurring of the boundaries and identity markers between people and groups. In chapter 3, we saw Jacob committing what may have been an irreparable breach in his relationship with the Nephites: he compared them unfavorably with their enemies, the Lamanites, saying that the Lamanites were more righteous (Jacob 3:3, 5–6) and had more conservative family

---

19. According to Clark Johnson, there are "only four temple discourses recorded in the Book of Mormon." Clark V. Johnson, "Jacob: In Harmony with God (Jacob 1–3, 7)," in *Studies in Scripture, Vol. 7: 1 Nephi to Alma 29*, ed. Kent P. Jackson (Salt Lake City: Deseret Book, 1987), 177.

20. See René Girard, *The Scapegoat*, trans. Yvonne Freccero (Baltimore: The Johns Hopkins University Press, 1986), 94.

values. Moreover, he told them that the Lamanites would destroy them with a scourge (v. 3), while the Lamanites themselves would be blessed and find favor with the Lord (v. 6).

We can imagine the people's anger rising against Jacob. Whose side was that priest on, anyway? Who was he to give them commandments (Jacob 3:9), tell them they were lousy parents (v. 10), and warn them to stop being "angels to the devil" (v. 11)? No wonder in Jacob 4 we see the priest retreating to his written record. Maybe Jacob is doing so only because he has become old and, like many people near the end of life, feels an urge to write a record for posterity. Or maybe it's something else, and he worries that the rift between himself and the people, or at least between himself and the king he has openly criticized, is great enough now that his life is in danger. He does not tell us, but there is a subtext in verse 14 of Jacob 4, when he speaks of how the Jews, "a stiffnecked people" who "despised the words of plainness," killed their prophets. Of his own people he has already said that he must speak the truth to them in "plainness" about their many sins. Does Jacob expect the same dark fate that has befallen other prophets?

A scapegoat is slandered and accused

If step 1 occurred because Jacob in his sacred role as priest and defender of the faith has alienated his people, Sherem comes into this situation as a convenient scapegoat who will reunite Jacob with the Nephites. At first glance, Sherem may seem an unlikely candidate for a scapegoat. He is not disabled or mad, two qualities that Girard posits as attractive because they signal weakness. He is not one of "those at the bottom of the social ladder," as Girard puts it.[21] On the other hand, he is also not at the very top of the social strata, rich and powerful, a visible target in the eye of the hurricane. He is not a king or an official priest to this people.

Still, that is the role he is attempting to play, which makes him potential prey. Sherem serves as a suitable scapegoat because he is enough like Jacob, the real focus of the people's likely anger, to become

---

21. Girard, *Scapegoat*, 18.

an acceptable substitute. Sherem desires to serve as both priest and prophet, Jacob's twin roles, and he is a deeply religious man. Both Sherem and Jacob also have the same goal: to win the hearts of the people. Moreover, he clearly comes from outside the community in some sense. He is a foreigner in their midst.

In step 2, the scapegoat must be slandered and accused, which Jacob does. He lays out the theological case against Sherem by alleging that Sherem has not understood the scriptures, which point to Christ. Even more significantly, he actually demonizes Sherem. Jacob makes a strong rhetorical move here, from first stating that Sherem was acting under "the power of the devil" in Jacob 7:4 to the ontological accusation, given in his face-to-face debate with Sherem in verse 14, that "thou art *of* the devil." Evil has gone in just ten verses from something that Sherem does to something that Sherem is. This, according to Girard, is not uncommon in scapegoating:

> The guilty person is so much a part of his offense that one is indistinguishable from the other. His defense seems to be a fantastic essence or ontological attribute. In many myths the wretched person's presence is enough to contaminate everything around him, infecting men and beasts with the plague, ruining crops, poisoning food, causing game to disappear, and sowing discord around him. Everything shrivels under his feet and the grass does not grow again. He produces disasters as easily as a fig tree produces figs. He need only be himself.[22]

Note that Sherem never launches the same accusation back at Jacob. Sherem believes Jacob has misunderstood the law and has been delinquent in his duties, but Sherem does not go so far as to anathematize his interlocutor.

---

22. Girard, *Scapegoat*, 36.

Evidence is presented that the scapegoat is guilty

Step 3 requires that the scapegoat be tried and found guilty, and inter-estingly enough, Jacob narrates this section so that he is not the one serving as the judge and jury. Jacob may be the prosecuting attorney in the initial cross-examination, asking leading theological questions to elicit Sherem's heresy, but Sherem hoists himself by his own petards here, admitting that he does not believe in the coming Christ (Jacob 7:9) and demanding a sign by the power of the Holy Ghost (v. 13).

Sherem's need for a sign from God is, ironically, what seems to seal his fate. In Jacob's eyes, even the fact that Sherem asks for a sign is evidence of his guilt. Jacob believes that Sherem secretly knows the teachings about Christ are true, but since Sherem is "of the devil" (Jacob 7:14), he's only going to deny that truth. What will be an unmistakable sign unto Sherem, Jacob suggests, will be the Lord's terrible smiting.

It isn't just Sherem's being struck down by the Lord that shows his guilt. When he recovers some days later, Sherem presents the evidence against himself by giving the people a helpful checklist of all of his past wrongs. In fact, Jacob has Sherem requesting a public audience just for this purpose. Jacob is more or less absent from that scene, not entering into the conversation at all as Sherem details how he denied the Christ, misunderstood the scriptures, and lied to God (Jacob 7:19).

The language Jacob uses to distantly describe this scene is telling. Note that in verses 17 and 18 Jacob says that Sherem "spake plainly unto them," which at first glance seems merely like a reversal of Sherem's previous pattern of flattery, but on deeper examination may reveal a hint about what is about to happen. Prophets who speak plainly have a distressing tendency to die. Just as Jacob once spoke plainly to the people about their sins, now Sherem speaks plainly about his own, making Sherem even more compelling as a stand-in for the sacrifice that is needed.

The scapegoat is convicted, killed, or banned

Sherem's sacrifice comes in step 4, when he gives up "the ghost." This act is dispensed with in a single verse, verse 20. Both the account's brevity and its ambiguity are intriguing from a Girardian point of view. It is actually unclear from the text just how Sherem dies or who is responsible for the execution. Has God struck Sherem down directly? Have the people done so, animated by the Spirit and the wrath of God? Or have the people killed Sherem of their own accord? The text does not tell us.

God had previously struck Sherem dumb, and Sherem was nourished "for the space of many days" while he came to terms with his theological errors (Jacob 7:15). That was a reckoning, but not a death. The Book of Mormon text never blames God for Sherem's death; if anyone is responsible, it seems to be Sherem himself, who surrenders his life force ("And it came to pass that when he had said these words he could say no more, and he gave up the ghost," Jacob 7:20). Girard notes that in stories of scapegoating, "the study of myths suggests that there was a very strong tendency, especially in Greek mythology, to minimize and even suppress the crimes of the gods."[23] This is part of a larger tendency to conceal collective violence. The ambiguity of Jacob 7 lends itself to this theory of suppression, as does the phrase "gave up the ghost"—especially since that is the expression the KJV uses to describe Jesus's final moments on the cross.

> And Jesus cried with a loud voice, and gave up the ghost. And the veil of the temple was rent in twain from the top to the bottom. And when the centurion, which stood over against him, saw that he so cried out, and gave up the ghost, he said, Truly this man was the Son of God. (Mark 15:37–39, KJV)

In the case of Jesus, death was a vicarious sacrifice to save humanity. It paved the way for sinful people to reconcile with God. The Sherem story, however, has much the same function, so the mirrored phrasing of "gave up the ghost" seems more than a literary coincidence. Sherem's death was not, like Jesus's, able to wipe out all human sin for all time.

---

23. Girard, *The Scapegoat*, 80.

It was, however, the catalyst for a single group of people to become reconciled to God, if only for a while.

Order is restored

It doesn't take long—just one verse—before step 5 is fully underway and order is restored. The people fall down in repentance, just like Sherem did. But unlike Sherem, the people don't have to die, because their scapegoat has already performed that function in their stead.

Sherem's death galvanizes the Nephite people to greater righteousness. Although after this chapter Sherem is never mentioned again, his effect on the people is clear: Nephite religion changes after his sacrificial death. Sharon Harris has noted a decided uptick in the use of the word faith, for example, after the small plates were recorded. The small plates account for 27 percent of the Book of Mormon, but only 10 percent of the use of the word *faith*, a word that becomes more important going forward.[24] After Sherem's death, the people are reconverted. They have not abandoned Mosaic law—Jacob says they "searched the scriptures" (Jacob 7:23), but they do so now with the love of God in their hearts.

Sherem's death also rebuilds the boundaries between civilizations, refortifying the identity differentiation between Nephite and Lamanite. Whereas in his temple sermon Jacob had blurred those once-sharp edges (step 1), calling the Lamanites righteous and blessed, after Sherem's death we return to the classic us-them formulation in which Nephite history depicts the Lamanites as wicked aggressors. In Jacob 7:24 Jacob says the Lamanites delighted in bloodshed and "sought by the power of their arms to destroy [the Nephites] continually." And in verse 25, the Nephites rise triumphant against these enemies, reassured once again that they are the good guys of history.

It's all thanks to Sherem, really. The man of God in this story has come not to vanquish but to be vanquished. His message, unlike that of the Hebrew Bible men of God, is not one of change. We noted earlier that in those stories the status quo is always upheld in regard to

---

24. See, Sharon Harris's essay, "Covenant Obligation to Scripture as Covenant Obligation to Family," included in this volume.

religion but usually reversed in regard to power. Monarchies come crashing down, and the people return to Mosaic law. In the Sherem story, this is exactly reversed: the priestly order remains the same—its inherited nature reinforced by Jacob's reference in his final verse to passing on the sacred record to his son Enos—but Nephite religion expands to encompass something new. Sherem's sacrificial death makes the Nephite people more than conquerors as they march into battle with God—and Jacob—on their side.

Reading Signs
or Repeating Symptoms

Adam S. Miller

The scene

Jacob and Sherem meet but never connect. They circle the same sun but on wildly divergent planes. This isn't unusual. People talk past each other all the time. Our meetings are framed and spaced by layers of circumstance, ignorance, and protocol. The things that worry me are not the things that interest you. What you'd hope to see in me isn't the profile I wanted to show. And so we feel alone even when we're together.

Some of this is our own fault, but some of it isn't. Part of the problem is language itself. Language helps put us in relation, but it also structures those relations. And language, in order to be dependable, must be predictable. The way verbs are conjugated, the way words are ordered, the way certain kinds of statements or questions solicit a certain kind of response—these regularities give language its consistency. But these regularities also give language its rigidity. These words and forms give shape to the lives that we share, but too, the mechanical character of that language invests all these ready-made words and prefabricated forms with a life of their own. They acquire an almost automatic character such that, rather than speaking a language, language often ends up speaking us.

Some of language's prefabricated forms are common and generic. Think of how greetings have a predictable formality. Or think of how the basic elements of a conversation between strangers at a party are already choreographed—the kinds of questions that can be asked, the kinds of answers that can be given. Most of what we say every day is just a slight variation on what we said yesterday.

But some of these prefabricated forms are very specific to each person. These specific forms are shaped by the details of our personal histories, the idiosyncrasies of our genealogies, and especially by the constellations of need and desire that structured our earliest relationships. The originally specialized patterns that structure these relationships—patterns that, to this day, situate me in a certain way with respect to my mother, that shape my expectations in relation to a friend, that make me hungry for my father's approval—end up functioning as general templates for my relationships with other people.

These specialized patterns get recycled as all-purpose widgets, and so I end up repeating with my boss elements of my relationship with my father, repeating with my wife elements of my relationship with my mother, repeating with my bishop elements of my relationship with my brother, etc. With some concretion, but generally with little awareness, these primal scenes get acted out again and again, automatically, mechanically, in my head, in my dreams, and in real life. At the heart of these scenes is a missing piece—a hole, a need—that fuels the drive to rigidly, symptomatically repeat them with whoever happens to be on hand.

Much of this repetition is futile: the hole never gets filled. But there is also a kind of utility here. Widely applied, the repetition of these scenes can make it easier to deal with people. Rather than needing to respond to the particulars, I can, without reflection, slot people into preassigned roles and then, focused on what I need, I can just respond to the generic features of the roles themselves. Rather than responding to you, I can respond to your role in the story I'm compelled—once again, today—to retell. In psychoanalysis this is called transference. In religion we often just call it sin. Sin: when we get bolted into patterns of transference that stubbornly keep us from seeing (and, thus, loving) someone else.

Jacob's symptom

A lot of what happens between Jacob and Sherem in Jacob 7 has this
feel. They talk right past each other. They can't quite see each other.
They don't respond to each other as people but as types. Their projec-
tions lock orbits, and their symptoms form a complementary pair.

Consider Jacob first. As Jacob narrates their encounter, the story
has a stark, didactic simplicity. Jacob is good and Sherem is bad. Where
Jacob displays "the power of the Lord" (Jacob 7:15), Sherem displays the
"power of the devil" (v. 4).[1] On the face of it, this isn't wrong. But there
is something disappointing about how this unfolds.

When Sherem confronts Jacob with a charge of blasphemy and
perversion, Jacob responds in kind. Throughout, Jacob appears more
interested in defending a certain kind of Christian doctrine than with
enacting a certain kind of Christian behavior. He seems invested in
and sharply limited by a certain pattern of speaking and thinking. To
be sure, Sherem does the same with Jacob. But where this is predictable
in Sherem's case, it feels tragic in Jacob's because the doctrine that
Jacob is defending does itself maintain that Christian behavior is more
important than any Christian ideas. The idea of Christ's love is not the
thing at stake. Christ's love is. It's true that Jacob defends the idea of
Christ's love with both force and effect, but it's also true that we hardly
see him enacting that love.

Sherem, we're told, "did lead away many hearts" from the doctrine of Christ (Jacob 7:3). But Jacob doesn't seek Sherem out. In fact,
Sherem has to go looking for Jacob and, apparently, has a hard time
finding him. Sherem, Jacob says, "sought much opportunity that he
might come unto me" (v. 3). Where is Jacob? Why is he so hard to
find? Why isn't he actively seeking out Sherem? Or, consider how
things play out during and after their confrontation. When Sherem
finds Jacob, he immediately levels an apparently sincere charge that
Jacob's doctrine of Christ is perverting the law of Moses and mislead-
ing the people. Sherem sees himself as defending God's law. Jacob isn't

---

1. All citations of Jacob 7 in this essay refer to Royal Skousen's critical edition of the
text, *The Book of Mormon: The Earliest Text* (New Haven: Yale University Press: 2009).

impressed. He responds with some leading questions, invites God to smite Sherem as a sign, and then (wham!) "the power of the Lord came upon [Sherem], insomuch that he fell to the earth" (v. 15). But immediately following this sign, Jacob again disappears from the text, and, in the aftermath, there is no mention of his being present to "nourish" Sherem as he lays stricken or of his being present to hear Sherem's deathbed confession. Essentially, Jacob shows up in the narrative only for the smiting itself.

Perhaps most telling, though, is Jacob's unquestioned confidence that Sherem's request for a sign is disingenuous. Jacob testifies that he knows, "by the power of the Holy Ghost," that "if there should be no atonement made, all mankind must be lost" (Jacob 7:12). Sherem asks for the same revelation: "Shew me a sign by this power of the Holy Ghost" (v. 13). But Jacob, without any hesitation, declares that, even if God were to show Sherem a sign, "thou wilt deny it because thou art of the devil" (v. 14). This is strong language and a boldly categorical prediction: even if the Holy Ghost were to intervene, Sherem will deny it, Jacob promises. There is no hope for Sherem.

But Jacob is wrong. The sign comes and—even though the sign comes in the form of a smiting—Sherem confesses Christ and repents. More, his testimony of Christ is sufficiently powerful that the multitude gathered to hear his testimony is "astonished exceedingly, insomuch that the power of God came down upon them and they were overcome, that they fell to the earth" (Jacob 7:21). In turn, this mass conversion is itself so profound that "peace and the love of God was restored again among the people" (v. 23). Sherem's deathbed preaching appears to be massively successful in a way that Jacob's own preaching was not.

But this isn't how Jacob frames it. Jacob undercuts any part Sherem may have had in sparking this transformation by claiming that these events happened because "I had requested it of my Father which was in heaven, for he had heard my cry and answered my prayer" (Jacob 7:22). Here, Jacob's prayers are assigned the role of prime mover, and Sherem won't be allowed out of the box Jacob has put him in. And so, with a final parting jab, Jacob baldly concludes the whole story by *still* referring to Sherem as "this wicked man" (v. 23).

Sherem's position

Much of Jacob's treatment of Sherem feels shortsighted and unfair. And though Jacob successfully defends the doctrine of Christ, he doesn't seem to do it in a very Christlike way. In fact, he defends the doctrine of Christ against the letter of the Mosaic law in a way that, in itself, seems in lockstep with the letter of the law. What's going on here? If Jacob is slotting Sherem into a prefabricated role in a scene that Jacob's own life compels him to replay, what role is this? What position does Sherem occupy?

Something about Sherem sets Jacob off. Something about him reopens an old wound. Jacob clearly bears such a wound. Only moments after recounting his unmitigated victory over Sherem, Jacob drifts right back into melancholy and tells us that, until his dying day, he mourned: "We did mourn out our days" (Jacob 7:26). What is the cause of Jacob's persistent mourning? What can't he put behind him? The Nephites, Jacob recounts, were "a lonesome and a solemn people, wanderers cast out from Jerusalem, born in tribulation in a wild wilderness, and hated of [their] brethren, which caused wars and contentions" (v. 26). Jacob is the bearer of this old wound, his father's wound, a family wound. He mourns for Jerusalem. He mourns for the loss of a city he never knew. But, for Jacob, this wound has some additional specificity. He is also "hated of [his] brethren," and this is not "brethren" in the abstract. As a first-generation Nephite, Jacob means something much more immediate: he means his actual brothers, Laman and Lemuel.

Jacob's lonesome tribulation in the wilderness is framed on the one hand by the loss of a city he never knew and, on the other, by the fact that his brothers hate him. The catalyst for both these losses is the same: the doctrine of Christ. From the start, Nephi reports, the Jews hated and "did mock [Lehi] because of the things which he testified of them" because he "testified that the things which he saw and heard, and also the things which he read in the book, manifested plainly of the coming of a Messiah and also the redemption of the world" (1 Nephi 1:19). And from the start, Nephi continues, Laman and Lemuel "were like unto [those] which were at Jerusalem" (1 Nephi 2:13).

These are the lines that frame Jacob's primal scene. And this is the scene that will, with a telling mechanicity, repeat itself not only in Jacob's life but for the next thousand years in the lives of his people—again and again, generation after generation—until the repetition itself destroys them all. When Jacob looks at Sherem, why can't he see him? I think the answer is straightforward. When Jacob looks at Sherem, all he can see is Laman and Lemuel. He can't engage with Sherem because, throughout their encounter, he's too busy shadowboxing his brothers.

Sherem, like Laman, Lemuel, and the people in Jerusalem, is a defender of the received tradition. In particular, Sherem, like Laman and Lemuel, is keen to defend the primacy of the law of Moses against the imposition of any novel dreams, visions, or messianic revelations. But these are, as Nephi noted, exactly the objections lodged by Laman and Lemuel against Lehi. "Thou art like unto our father," they tell Nephi, "led away by the foolish imaginations of his heart. . . . And we know that the people which were in the land of Jerusalem were a righteous people, for they keep the statutes and judgments of the Lord and all his commandments according to the law of Moses; wherefore we know that they are a righteous people" (1 Nephi 17:20, 22). Sherem mirrors exactly these claims:

> And ye have led away much of this people, that they pervert the right way of God and keep not the law of Moses, which is the right way, and convert the law of Moses into the worship of a being which ye say shall come many hundred years hence. And now behold, I Sherem declare unto you that this is blasphemy, for no man knoweth of such things; for he cannot tell of things to come. (Jacob 7:7)

On Sherem's account, the "law of Moses" is itself the "right way of God," not a shadow of it, not a sign of things to come. For Sherem, Jacob's doctrine of Christ looks beyond the mark and ignores the plainness of the law. It "converts" the law of Moses into an apparatus for worshipping a future messiah, and, as a result, it interferes with the law's operation in structuring and ordering their everyday lives and relationships.

It is on this score that Sherem's position is more consistent than Jacob's. Sherem's position that the law is what structures and orders our relationship to the world is consistent with his own willingness to submit to and massage the structures imposed by language. But Jacob's willingness to do the same is not consistent with the doctrine of Christ he's defending. Sherem is a master of the law. And in particular, he is a master of how the law organizes our desires and locks us into repeating certain scenes. Sherem, Jacob tells us, "was learned, that he had a perfect knowledge of the language of the people; wherefore he could use much flattery and much power of speech according to the power of the devil" (Jacob 7:4). Sherem's learning and power are pegged directly to his "perfect knowledge of the language of the people." He understands how language works, he recognizes the constraints that language imposes, and he knows that, at the heart of our compulsion to repeat these primal scenes, there is a wound, a need, a desire. Sherem recognizes these templates as symptoms. As a result, Sherem can position himself in a way that is flattering to the stories that people need to repeat.

This is what flattery amounts to: the power to position yourself as a willing mirror for whatever image others hope to see reflected back to them. In this sense, flattery isn't just a name for a certain way of speaking; it's a general name for smoothly functioning transference. When flattery succeeds, it creates order. It gathers people up. It stabilizes the images we project onto each other. Flattery shows us what we want to see. It reflects back to us what we expected. When this happens, a reassuring consistency reigns. But this compelled, mechanical consistency is also quite stifling and, ultimately, lonely. A regulated economy of mirror images is exhilarating but empty.

This is where Jacob and Sherem find themselves: hamstrung by flattery. They are compelled by their wounds to repeat complementary scenes, scenes that bind them together as a pair of prefabricated images but prevent them from connecting as people. Sherem doesn't address Jacob, he addresses only a "lawbreaker." And Jacob doesn't address Sherem, he addresses only a "Christ-denier." Though adversarial, these roles collude to reinforce the mutual exclusion of the actual people attached to them.

Signs from heaven

What, then, can be done? It's not as if we could do without these struc-tures that order and regulate our relationships. It's not as if we could do without law and language. Without law and language we would be even more isolated and alone than we are when we're trapped within their confines. What we need, rather, is a doctrine of Christ that can enact a new relation to the law, a doctrine that can retain these structures but give us room to move in relation to them.

The key to this doctrine of Christ is a spirit of prophecy that can read the law itself as sign. Rather than just repeating it as a symp-tom, a spirit of prophecy can read in the staging of a primal scene the truth about the too-human wound that compels the repetition in the first place. This spirit can, as Jacob puts it, recognize that "none of the prophets have written nor prophesied save they have spoken concern-ing this Christ" (Jacob 7:11).

Now, at one level, what Jacob claims about scripture is clearly false. Most of scripture is straightforwardly, like the law itself, about something *other* than Christ. In order to point to Christ, the law and prophets must themselves be read as signs that, at heart, testify to the truth of the world's original wound and, especially, to the manifesta-tion of Christ in that wound as the lamb slain from the foundation of the world (cf. Revelation 13:8). This is the doctrine of Christ:

> And notwithstanding we believe in Christ, we keep the law of Moses and look forward with steadfastness unto Christ until the law shall be fulfilled, for for this end was the law given. Wherefore the law hath become dead unto us, and we are made alive in Christ because of our faith, yet we keep the law because of the command-ments. And we talk of Christ, we rejoice in Christ, we preach of Christ, we prophesy of Christ; and we write according to our prophecies that our children may know to what source they may look for a remission of their sins. Wherefore we speak concerning the law, that our children may know the deadness of the law. And they,

> by knowing the deadness of the law, may look forward
> unto that life which is in Christ and know for what end
> the law was given. (2 Nephi 25:24–27)

The law must be kept and its structures preserved, but they must be kept in such a way that they become "dead unto us." When this happens, the spell is broken.

In sin, the law takes on a life of its own and *we* feel dead in relation to it. We feel excluded from our own lives and isolated from other people. But the doctrine of Christ inverts this scenario. When the law becomes dead, when the law no longer has a life of its own, when it loses its automatic and mechanical character, then we discover a new life in Christ. We're freed from sin. We're no longer locked into repeating the same futile, bloodless scenes. The key again is that the law must start functioning as a sign. We have to learn to read the performance of these scenes not, like Sherem, as a symptom available for manipulation but, like a prophet, as a sign that displays the human wounds that animate them.

This is hard to do. The templates that structure our relationships are themselves a defensive gesture meant to compensate for the wound that compels them. But there is here a general lesson to be drawn from Sherem's own experience of a sign. When signs come, they inevitably come, to one degree or another, as they did for Sherem. As Jacob puts it: "If God shall smite thee, let that be a sign unto thee" (Jacob 7:14). Every sign is smiting. Every sign that reveals Christ reveals him by touching the wound that we have been working to conceal. These signs break the tight circle of transference, of collusion and vanity. They collapse our prearranged games. They open us to something beyond the prefabricated scenes and ready-made meanings we work so hard to impose on the world. And they make room for these scenes to be redeployed, instead, as signs of the very wounds they'd been hiding. Signs open us to the possibility of revelation, ministering angels, prophecies, visions, and dreams. Signs, revealing the doctrine of Christ, open us to the possibility of a world where we are not alone.

Reclamation

In conclusion, allow me to speculate on a final point. When God smites Sherem such that he falls to the earth, this is a sign. But, it seems to me, this sign isn't just for Sherem. This sign is also meant for Jacob. Granted, the sign wakes Sherem up such that he "confessed the Christ and the power of the Holy Ghost and the ministering of angels" (Jacob 7:17). But the sign gives Jacob a bracing shake as well. It may be true that Jacob never truly sees Sherem—Sherem dies before he really has a chance—but Jacob clearly signals that, even if he never manages to see Sherem, Sherem has put him in a position to see Laman and Lemuel again.

Note that after Sherem confesses Christ and "the love of God" is restored among the people, Jacob immediately turns his attention to the Lamanites: "And it came to pass that many means were devised to reclaim and restore the Lamanites to the knowledge of the truth" (Jacob 7:24). These efforts fail, but the fact that Jacob is moved to *try* is significant. When he looked at Sherem, Jacob could see only the ghosts of Laman and Lemuel. He saw these ghosts so clearly that he was sure that even if God gave Sherem a sign, Sherem (like Laman and Lemuel) would harden his heart and never repent.

But the sign came and Sherem *did* repent. He did confess Christ. And then something happens to Jacob. For the first time in decades, Jacob can see his own brothers more clearly. He can see Laman and Lemuel, not as players in his story but as flesh-and-blood people. For the first time in decades, Jacob can read in their anger the wound that compelled *them* to repeat their own primal scene. Then, for the first time in decades, Jacob dares to hope that his brothers aren't lost forever. This is the doctrine of Christ.

The Lord's Prayer(s) in Jacob 7

Kimberly M. Berkey

THE PLOT OF JACOB 7 IS FAIRLY WELL-KNOWN among Latter-day Saints, at least in its broad contours: a meddlesome antichrist confronts the Nephite prophet and is fatally struck down by a sign from heaven, delivering with his dying breath a confession so stirring that it over-whelms the attendant crowds, who devote themselves once more to peace and righteous living. The vividness of this narrative, combined with its straightforwardly moralistic assessment of its primary char-acters, renders Jacob 7 a particularly attractive resource for didactic purposes—a use evident in devotional treatments of this chapter but also witnessed in the way the Book of Mormon redeploys elements of Jacob 7 in its later narrative, thus fashioning the concluding chapter of Jacob's record into a kind of type-scene for subsequent portions of Nephite history.[1]

---

1. I have in mind primarily Alma 30, which contains a host of verbal allusions to Jacob 7, and 3 Nephi 1, in which Nephite multitudes fall to the earth after witnessing a sign. The similarities between Jacob 7 and Alma 30 are usually treated thematically rather than verbally as part of the triple comparison of Sherem, Nehor, and Korihor. See Brigham D. Madsen, "B. H. Roberts's Studies of the Book of Mormon," *Dialogue* 26/3 (1993): 77–86; Mark D. Thomas, "Dying Heretics," in *Digging in Cumorah: Reclaim-ing Book of Mormon Narratives* (Salt Lake City: Signature Books, 1999), 161–71; and John W. Welch, "Comparing Sherem, Nehor, and Korihor," in *The Legal Cases in the Book of Mormon* (Provo, UT: Brigham Young University Press and the Neal A. Maxwell Institute for Religious Scholarship, 2008), 301–9.

But behind the scenes, backstage to the compelling drama of Sherem's confrontation with Jacob and the ecstatic collapse of the Nephite audience, we find the more subdued and generally neglected figure of a praying priest. Twice in this chapter Jacob prays, and twice in response a person or group of people falls to the earth. In the course of this double supplication, it also seems that Jacob learns something vital about prayer since his two prayers are marked by a certain tension in how each treats the role of the will. Crucially, the chapter illustrates this tension by the way it incorporates, recontextualizes, and reorders two of Jesus's prayers from the New Testament. What follows in this paper, then, is an extended comparison of Jacob 7:14 with Jacob 7:22 in order to illustrate the way in which Sherem's collapse calls Jacob to repentance and fundamentally alters his approach to prayer.

Jacob's two prayers are found at the core of the chapter, framing Sherem's confession and death, and each is tied to the unfolding drama as a kind of causal force. In the first instance, the heaven-sent sign that ultimately sends Sherem to his death occurs pointedly *not* after Sherem's snide demand ("Shew me a sign by this power of the Holy Ghost, in the which ye know so much," Jacob 7:13)[2] but after Jacob's petitioning response in the following verse:

> What am I that I should tempt God to show unto thee a sign in the thing which thou knowest to be true? Yet thou wilt deny it because thou art of the devil. Nevertheless not my will be done; but if God shall smite thee, let that be a sign unto thee that he hath power both in heaven and in earth and also that Christ shall come. And thy will, O Lord, be done and not mine. (Jacob 7:14)

With these words, Sherem immediately "fell to the earth" and required "nourish[ment] for the space of many days" (Jacob 7:15). He eventually gathers a group of Nephites around his deathbed and recants point by point his earlier assertions (vv. 17, 19), after which the group

---

2. I have used Royal Skousen's *The Book of Mormon: The Earliest Text* (New Haven: Yale University Press, 2009) as my base text for Book of Mormon quotations.

of onlookers was so "overcome" that they too "fell to the earth" (v. 21). Although Jacob had been oddly absent from the confession narrative to this point, the resulting collective experience of the people is not something he can let pass without comment, and so Jacob reemerges as a named and active character precisely in order to take credit for the people's response: "Now this thing was pleasing unto me Jacob, for I had requested it of my Father which was in heaven, for he had heard my cry and answered my prayer" (v. 22).

The fact that Jacob narrates this prayer only retroactively is significant because it demonstrates the careful construction of the confession scene. Mentions of prayer both begin and end this pericope, a frame that would have been interrupted had Jacob narrated his second prayer in its proper chronological order. Viewed in this light, the scene of Sherem's confession appears deliberately structured, clearly placing each of Jacob's prayers on the outer edge of a chiastic setting (Jacob 7:14–22):

A Jacob's first prayer (v. 14)
  B Sherem falls to the earth (v. 15)
    C Sherem anticipates his death (v. 16)
      D Confession (vv. 17–19)
    C' Sherem dies (Jacob v. 20)
  B' The people fall to the earth (v. 21)
A' Jacob's second prayer (v. 22)

This parallel structural position is not the only commonality between the two prayers, however. These verses are also linked verbally in the way they echo phrases from Jesus's most famous prayers recorded in the New Testament.[3] Jacob's first prayer shares the language of Jesus's words in Gethsemane when he pled with God to "remove this cup from me: nevertheless not my will, but thine, be done" (Luke 22:42).

---

3. This is not the first time Jacob's record alludes to the New Testament. Elizabeth Fenton notes that Jacob 5 seems to develop imagery drawn from Romans 11:24 such that "the parable of the olive tree not only describes grafting but also operates as a kind of grafting itself." Elizabeth Fenton, "Open Canons: Sacred History and American History in *The Book of Mormon*," *Journal of Nineteenth-Century Americanists* 1/2 (Fall 2013): 344.

In a parallel too overt to miss, Jacob likewise sacrifices his preference with the words "nevertheless not my will be done" and then repeats this sentiment a few lines later, this time also incorporating a positive affirmation of God's will: "Thy will, O Lord, be done and not mine" (Jacob 7:14). Perhaps more subtly, Jacob's second prayer echoes another famous moment of Jesus in conversation with the Father, this time from the model prayer presented in the Sermon on the Mount, in which Jesus begins, "Our Father which art in heaven" (Matthew 6:9). Likewise, Jacob includes in his second prayer specific reference to God's location: "I had requested it of my Father which was in heaven" (Jacob 7:22). In the two instances in this chapter where Jacob narrates his prayers, the text invokes clear liturgical and theological echoes for its Christian readers by quoting phrases they will recognize from the New Testament.

In some ways, putting the prayer in Gethsemane in conversation with the Lord's Prayer is hardly a surprising move, since at least one of the Gospels seems to stage the comparison already. Matthew grants these prayers structural significance by using them to bookend Jesus's ministry and by stressing their semantic resemblance. Jesus declares "thy will be done" only twice in Matthew's Gospel—once in the Lord's Prayer (Matthew 6:10) and once in the Gethsemane prayer (Matthew 26:42).[4] By placing these two prayers in parallel, Jacob 7 is picking up on a close relationship already signaled within the New Testament.

And yet there seem to be two primary oddities about Jacob 7's incorporation of Jesus's prayers. First is the way the chapter seems to deliberately mute their most obvious parallel. The structure of the confession scene encourages us to compare verses 14 and 22 side by side,

---

4. This commonality is amply noted in commentaries on these verses. W. D. Davies and Dale C. Allison, *The Gospel according to Saint Matthew*, International Critical Commentary 26 (Edinburgh: T&T Clark, 1988), 1:605; 3:500; Donald A. Hagner, *Matthew 14–28*, Word Biblical Commentary 33B (Dallas: Word Books, 1995), 784; John Nolland, *The Gospel of Matthew*, New International Greek Testament Commentary 1 (Grand Rapids, MI: Eerdmans, 2005), 288, 1103; R. T. France, *The Gospel of Matthew*, New International Commentary on the New Testament (Grand Rapids, MI: Eerdmans, 2007), 1006; Ulrich Luz, *Matthew*, Hermeneia, trans. James E. Crouch (Minneapolis: Fortress Press, 2007), 44:319, 46:397.

yet when verse 22 quotes the Lord's Prayer, rather than highlighting the already inherent commonality of the source texts behind these two verses (the phrase "thy will be done"), it echoes the fairly banal opening line, "My Father which was in heaven." If Jacob 7 wants to suggest a comparison of these two New Testament prayers, why does it drop their most overt point of commonality? The second oddity is the inverted order of the Lord's Prayer and the Gethsemane prayer within Jacob 7. The story line of the Gospels, which traces an arc from Jesus's early ministry to his betrayal and death, seems poised to privilege the climactic events surrounding the end of Jesus's life, including his last recorded prayer uttered in Gethsemane. If, as many readers have assumed, the New Testament thus implicitly privileges the Gethsemane prayer, what significance might we find in the fact that Jacob 7 seems to trace the opposite arc, beginning instead with the Gethsemane prayer in verse 14 and moving toward the Lord's Prayer in verse 22 as the climactic instance of supplication? If we want to posit an implicit theology of prayer in Jacob 7, these seem to be the primary questions to keep in mind.

There are thus three main parallels between the prayers in Jacob 7:14 and Jacob 7:22: both frame the central drama of Sherem's confession, both echo Jesus's most famous prayers from the New Testament, and, as already noted above, both incite an identical result (the respective collapses of Sherem and the people). But if the several commonalities between these two verses justify examining them side by side, close comparison also reveals a series of tensions that are just as significant as their earlier points of convergence.

We might first note the opposing portrayal of God in each prayer. In verse 14 God is a figure of smiting and power, someone Jacob is concerned about "tempt[ing]" or provoking, and in the face of whose sovereignty Jacob takes on an abject, creaturely posture by asking not "*Who* am I that I should tempt God?" but rather "*What* am I?" By verse 22, however, God is given the title "Father" (the only familial designation out of fifteen total references to God in this chapter) and moreover is a father to whom Jacob feels free to make entreaties, which are then heard and answered. There is a striking shift, then, from a tone of servility in verse 14 to a tone of intimacy with God in verse 22, and this shift—from a sovereign "God" to a listening "Father," from worries about tempting God to straightforwardly entreating him—accompanies a second shift in how Jacob treats the topic of the will.

In verse 14, Jacob is particularly anxious about the place and role of his will. He moves from denying it ("not my will be done") to affirming God's will ("thy will, O Lord, be done") before returning once again to negate his own desires a second time ("not mine"). It is as if Jacob is caught in an iterative wrestle with his will, anxiously trying to delineate boundaries between the various desires that want to have sway in this situation. Jacob wants to ensure that there is space here for God's will to direct the possible outcomes that follow from Sherem's demand for a sign, but it seems that he has difficulty suppressing his own potentially opposing will. He no sooner affirms God's will than his own desires emerge a second time and must be wrestled back again. By verse 22, however, Jacob no longer appears conflicted. Although the Lord's Prayer, to which this verse alludes, does contain discussion of the will, it does so only by affirming "thy will be done" without any corresponding negation of the disciple's desire. And since this affirmation of God's will is only distantly implied and never explicitly invoked in verse 22, Jacob seems to have overcome certain anxieties he felt earlier about the role of his will. Indeed, Jacob has been so completely reconciled to his will that he actively issues a "request" and admits to its outcome as "pleasing," a behavior and an affect that imply a commitment to one's own desires.

Or to frame this shift in the treatment of "will" from another angle, we might also compare the frustrated tone of Jacob's prayer in verse 14 with the relative sincerity on display in verse 22. Jacob begins his response in verse 14 by describing unilaterally what he takes to be the stakes of Sherem's demand for a sign. Jacob refuses to "tempt God to shew unto thee a sign" because he is convinced that Sherem's request is insincere—a heavenly portent would only signify "the thing which thou knowest to be true" and, in any case, "thou wilt deny it because thou art of the devil" (Jacob 7:14). It is only here, after having laid out what he takes to be the unambiguous reality of the situation, that Jacob begins to echo Jesus's words: "Nevertheless, not my will be done." Read in context, this echo is less a sincere attempt to find out God's will and rather functions as Jacob's exit from the conversation. He is, in effect, throwing up his hands in frustration and absolving himself of any responsibility for the outcome. Although Jacob echoes Jesus's words, he seems to lack the intent associated with the Gethsemane prayer, instead replacing the sincerity of Jesus's original pronouncement with the detachment of Pilate's infamous handwashing (Matthew 27:24). "If God shall smite [Sherem]" (v. 14), that's well and good, but Jacob wants no part of it. By the time we reach verse 22, however, Jacob is praying sincerely and actively, a far cry from the frustration and self-willed passivity of his first prayer. Instead of simply absenting himself by attempting to remove his will, Jacob here issues a straightforward "request," and instead of leaving the outcome up to God to do whatever he pleases, in verse 22 Jacob makes a specific entreaty that requires his careful attention to and engagement with the situation in which he finds himself.

We might then summarize the shifts between verses 14 and 22 as follows. Where Jacob is in the first prayer abject before God and anxious about his own will, he appears in the second prayer to be in a much more intimate relationship with God as "Father" and not at all conflicted regarding his own desires. Additionally, where the first prayer demonstrates Jacob's frustrated wish to be uninvolved (he negates his will in order to absolve himself of responsibility), the second prayer shows him actively concerned, attending to his will as what allows him specific engagement with the situation at hand. In the space of less than ten verses, it seems that something fundamental has changed Jacob's orientation to God and to his own will. What, then, has changed Jacob, and how?

The most dramatic moment in the intervening verses between these prayers, and thus the most likely place to look for answers, is of course the sign given to Sherem and his immediate collapse. We can speculate about what that moment revealed to Jacob and then trace the shifts between his two prayers back to what he learned from this sign. Recall that when Jacob initially refused Sherem's demand for a sign, he did so on two grounds: first, his confidence in Sherem's duplicity, and second, his conviction that a sign would be ineffectual since Sherem would simply deny it. That early self-assurance, however, must have been abruptly shattered as soon as Jacob spoke the words "thy will, O Lord, be done" and witnessed his opponent's collapse. In an instant, Jacob comes to the dreadful realization that God *did* intend to smite Sherem after all, that Sherem *would* repent after receiving a sign, and that the only thing standing in the way of that sign's occurrence had been Jacob's unwillingness to invoke it. In short, Jacob is shown in dramatic fashion how he had misunderstood the stakes of his confrontation with Sherem.

I want to suggest that Jacob also came to a realization about his will in the course of this profoundly humbling moment. At a first, too-hasty glance, it would seem that Sherem's collapse drives home to Jacob the problematic status of his will, since the event demonstrates how Jacob's desires had run counter to God's intention to smite Sherem. But it is just as clear from verse 14 that Jacob had already recognized this problematic tension—after all, this is precisely the disparity he was trying to resolve by saying, "Not my will be done." Jacob *already* knew that his will and God's will were likely at odds or he would never have attempted to negate his own will in the first place. Thus, what Jacob learns at this moment is not something about the problematic status of his will (a fact already tacitly known), but rather he realizes that he had sought to resolve that tension in the wrong way.

Jacob's solution to the disparity between his will and God's will was to assume a self-imposed passivity, to negate his desires and effectively get out of God's way. Taking this approach, he too hastily resolved the ambiguity between his will and God's by endeavoring to subtract his own. What he may have realized, however, is that negating his own will was an insufficient gesture. If simply disavowing one's wishes was adequate to enact God's will, we might have expected the sign to occur midway through verse 14 when Jacob said "nevertheless, not my will be done." In actuality, however, it was not until Jacob had additionally *affirmed* God's will that the sign occurred. The moment that finally invoked God's power was the same moment that Jacob switched from referring to God in the third person ("if God shall smite thee") to directly addressing him ("O Lord"), the moment when Jacob was at his most active and prayerful. As Sherem hit the ground, Jacob recognized that something about his words and active involvement proved crucial to accomplishing God's will.

In sum, Jacob had misapprehended the nature of prayer. He seemed to understand prayer in verse 14 to be an arena for wrestling his will out of the way, turning prayer into a conflict between his will and God's will and inadvertently rendering God as his opponent. It was this conception of prayer that introduced the distance and servility noted above ("What am I that I should tempt God?"). Jacob realizes, however, that he is more than just a potential obstruction to God's will and that in fact his prayer can be a vital medium for realizing divine power. Although there may indeed be a disparity between Jacob's will and God's will, prayer is not primarily intended to address that discrepancy.

According to Jacob 7, there is instead an entirely different disparity that prayer attempts to address, and this is demonstrated in a curious convergence between verse 14 and verse 22. Although the chapter deliberately mutes the original resonance of the phrase "thy will be done" between the Lord's Prayer and the Gethsemane prayer, it appears to have done so in order to replace it with a different resonance. When these prayers are incorporated in Jacob 7, the chapter adds one small phrase that reconfigures the way Jacob's two prayers interact. After admitting that God may intend to smite Sherem despite Jacob's own pessimism about the effectiveness of such a gesture, Jacob outlines what he hopes this portent would communicate: "Let that be a sign unto thee that [God] has power both in heaven and in earth" (v. 14). Although easily overlooked because of the more obvious echoes of the Gethsemane prayer on either side, Jacob's mention of "heaven and . . . earth" seems to anticipate the reference in the Lord's Prayer to God's will having sway "in earth, as . . . in heaven" (Matthew 6:10), and this may help explain why verse 22 quotes such an oddly prosaic portion of the Lord's Prayer rather than one of its more familiar and seemingly more potent lines. When Jacob says that he prays to "my Father which was in heaven" (Jacob 7:22), the emphasis on God's location, "in heaven," directs the reader's attention back to the "heaven and . . . earth" reference in verse 14.[5] The chapter thus seems to indicate that, although there is a disparity at the heart of prayer, it is not the disparity between

---

5. This same allusion also highlights the double emphasis on "earth" in the intervening confession scene in which Sherem's collapse sends him specifically "to the earth"

divine and mortal wills, as Jacob had initially assumed. Rather, the disparity that prayer most fundamentally addresses is a disparity of *location.*

As it turns out, Jacob is no stranger to the importance of this division. The discrepancy between heaven and earth is, in fact, absolutely crucial to his broader theology. Like so much of his theology, Jacob's interest in the heaven/earth divide seems to have its genesis in the parting words of his father, Lehi, whose teachings on mortality and redemption are recorded in 2 Nephi 2. Midway through that chapter, Lehi testifies to his sons that "there is a God, and he hath created all things, both the heavens and the earth" (2 Nephi 2:14), an assertion that, on its surface, seems entirely straightforward. Just a few verses later, however, Lehi's assertion is recast in dramatically spatial terms when he describes "an angel" who "had fallen from heaven" (v. 17). In Lehi's final sermon to his family, an event that is formative for Jacob's later theology, the devil is introduced as someone who has traversed the divide between heaven and earth and remains confined to the mortal world. That same devil, Lehi goes on, entices the first humans to follow a similar course when, as a consequence of eating the forbidden fruit, Adam and Eve are cast out of the divine garden "to till the earth" (v. 19). This earthbound mortality then gives rise to one of Jacob's principal theological obsessions: the status of the flesh. Nothing seems to strike existential horror in Jacob like the thought that "this flesh must . . . crumble to its mother earth, to rise no more" (2 Nephi 9:7), and although we typically hear in this "rising" little more than the standard scriptural image for resurrection, it may also articulate an interest in actual vertical movement. For Jacob, the problem of the flesh is precisely its restriction to the earth: how can something mortal and corruptible ever regain a share in the divinity and perfection that redemption seems to require? What are we to do, in other words, in the face of the disparity between heaven and earth?

The solution to this dilemma is the coming Christ, a being who quite literally incorporates elements of both divinity and mortality in

---

and in which the attendant Nephite crowds are similarly so "overcome" that they "fell to the earth" (Jacob 7:15, 21).

order to overcome the division between them. In fact, articulating the soteriological role of Christ in terms of this discrepancy may explain why Jacob designates God's "power . . . in heaven and in earth" as the primary information a sign would communicate to Sherem, relegating the testimony "that Christ shall come" to second place (Jacob 7:14). Sherem must first fathom the spatial backdrop in which God's power operates in order to understand the salvific trajectory of the coming Christ. It is safe to say, at the very least, that for Jacob the divide between heaven and earth is vital and forms perhaps the central question of his entire theology.

And yet despite all the importance he ascribes to the heaven/earth disparity and his commitment to the coming messiah as its primary solution, Jacob seems ironically to have missed certain practical implications of this theology for his own discipleship and ministry. There is perhaps no role more suited to reflecting about one's responsibility to mediate heavenly power on earth than the role of Israelite temple priest, and yet Jacob appears to have problematically withdrawn from certain components of his earthly ministry.[6] There are clues in Jacob's record, for instance, that he gradually retreated from the public sphere and understood his role to be oriented primarily around his record and its future audience rather than around his contemporary Nephite brethren. After recording one of his public sermons in Jacob 1–3, the fourth chapter of his record opens with an extended reflection on the nature of engraving on metal plates (Jacob 4:1–2) and his purpose in writing (vv. 3–4), followed by direct exhortation to his readers (vv. 10–18). Jacob seems to have shifted rather suddenly from a public project of direct preaching to a written project, no longer recording his sermons or his public ministry but instead reflecting on the purpose of the plates, his hopes for his future readers, and his copying over of the allegory of

<hr />

6. Jacob's priestly appointment is mentioned in 2 Nephi 5:26 and Jacob 1:18. John W. Welch speculates about the added legal and ritual resonance that a temple setting would afford to the confrontation between Jacob and Sherem. See "The Case of Sherem," in *The Legal Cases of the Book of Mormon* (Provo, UT: BYU Press and Neal A. Maxwell Institute, 2008), 107–38; and "The Temple in the Book of Mormon: The Temples at the Cities of Nephi, Zarahemla, and Bountiful," in *Temples of the Ancient World*, ed. Donald W. Parry (Salt Lake City: Deseret Book, 1994), 309, 339.

Zenos like a dutiful scribe (Jacob 5). Perhaps the reason Sherem must "[seek] much opportunity" (Jacob 7:6) to find Jacob is that Jacob has, in some sense, retreated from his public role among the people.[7] Even when he reemerges into the public sphere in the narrative of chapter 7, Jacob seems marginal, difficult to find, and his posture remains almost entirely passive—so passive, in fact, that during Sherem's repentance and confession (arguably the most important scene in the chapter), Jacob is so far removed from the event that he narrates his own pivotal prayer outside the pericope altogether. Jacob's record has subtly communicated his steady retreat from among the people, who presumably did not take kindly to the stern rebuke of his opening sermon, and it is not hard to imagine that Jacob may have decided to confine himself to his somewhat sequestered role as temple priest (Jacob 1:17–18).

Has Jacob tried to confine himself, then, to heavenly things? Has he misunderstood his priestly role as primarily a question of holy aloofness from his people instead of atoning for and reuniting with them through the rituals of the Israelite temple—rituals that were intended, after all, to mediate Jehovah's heavenly holiness to his chosen people on earth? Perhaps the moment of the sign in verse 15 convicts Jacob as much as it had convicted Sherem, reminding him that discipleship is not a question of ascetically removing oneself to contemplate heaven but of making God's will and power incarnate on earth. By confining himself to the heavenly role of temple priest and reifying the distance between himself and his people, Jacob may have inadvertently denied his relationship with and responsibility for the messy and even profane situation on earth.

This brings us full circle to a reflection on how Jacob approaches himself and his will in prayer. In light of his broader theology and what we have seen in this chapter about the role of the will, Jacob may see his

---

7. Sherem's odd admission that he "sought much opportunity" to find Jacob is also a key feature of the discussion surrounding Sherem's ethnic identity. See Kevin Christensen, "The Deuteronomist De-Christianizing of the Old Testament," *FARMS Review* 16/2 (2004): 59–90; Brant A. Gardner, *Second Witness: Analytical and Contextual Commentary on the Book of Mormon* (Salt Lake City: Greg Kofford Books, 2007), 2:565–66; A. Keith Thompson, "Who Was Sherem?" *Interpreter: A Journal of Mormon Scripture* 14 (2015): 1–15.

earthly embodiment as, at root, a *problem*. If his embodiment is seen as a problem, prayer may then be seen as the solution. In this light, we might reconfigure what Jacob learned at Sherem's collapse as follows: although he had previously affirmed that God "hath power both in heaven and in earth" (Jacob 7:14), Jacob comes to see that God's possession of that power is somehow insufficient to equally accomplish the divine will in both realms. The full expression of God's power requires Jacob's prayer in order to be accomplished, and writing himself out of the situation by negating his own will hadn't helped. In fact, by praying with a focus on his will as part of the problem, praying as an abject creature tentatively estimating the claims of a distant sovereign, Jacob would have inadvertently reified the very disparity that prayer was meant to address. If the object of prayer is to overcome the distance between heaven and earth, it was not Jacob's opposing will that had nearly obstructed the miraculous sign but the distance he had imposed between earth and heaven by refiguring the relationship of creature and creator as a contest of wills.

When Jacob's prayer focused on the problem of negating his own will, it was ultimately motivated by a self-centered anxiety that ironically reinforced the very difficulty he hoped to resolve. Because Jacob took prayer to be a question of negating his will, prayer became an internal, affective project rather than an external, spatially oriented task. What Jacob comes to learn and enact by verse 22 is that his desires are not the point of prayer, whether he takes a positive or negative stance toward those desires. Jacob's task, rather, is to assume a certain mediating role on earth in order to help enact God's will "in earth, as it is in heaven" (Matthew 6:10). That mediation is possible only when he views himself more as God's colleague than God's vassal. After all, mankind was formed from "the dust of the ground" and given stewardship over the world (Genesis 2:7, 15; Moses 2:28)—made out of earth in order to tend the earth. By fretting over the status of his mortal will and retreating from his earthly stewardship over his people, Jacob may have misunderstood the individual and practical stakes of the heaven/earth divide.

In this respect, Jacob's second prayer is a far cry from his earlier aloofness and frustration. Here we find him actively and sincerely involved in the circumstance at hand, attending to the ways God might leverage the potential of this situation to manifest his divine power and then submitting that idea to God in the form of a specific "request" (Jacob 7:22). God is no longer a distant and terrifying sovereign, but instead a "Father" and a partner. And although the full text of the Lord's Prayer is only echoed in verse 22 rather than quoted, we might reflect at least briefly on how that prayer treats the will. In the Lord's Prayer, the disciple affirms only "thy will be done" without explicitly negating his own will, and this affirmative, tranquil attitude toward desire seems to match Jacob's general disposition in verse 22. God's will has been removed from any relation of dialectical antagonism with Jacob's, as was the case in verse 14. By verse 22 "thy will be done" is now something Jacob can seek in its own right. Jacob is content to let his will be checked in his pursuit of the larger project: prayer as a means to close the distance between heaven and earth. Jacob thus figures a type of prayer that acts as a conduit to convey God's will down to earth, rather than conveying his will (positive or negative) up to heaven.

With this in mind, we may have also arrived at an explanation for the chronological inversion of the two New Testament prayers in Jacob 7, an inversion that places the Lord's Prayer after the Gethsemane prayer. Although there is something unquestionably vital about Jesus's words in Gethsemane for what they teach about the potentially obstructive character of the human will, it may be significant that the model of prayer Jacob finally comes around to in verse 22—and thus the model of prayer that the chapter ultimately privileges—is the very same model Jesus himself explicitly privileged with the command, "After *this* manner therefore pray ye" (Matthew 6:9, emphasis added). The New Testament gives us the Lord's Prayer as the explicit model we should follow, perhaps because the Lord's Prayer more clearly models the stance a disciple must take toward his or her own will.

Jacob 7 shows not only that Christ came to heal the gap between heaven and earth (Jacob 7:11–12, 14), but that we can obstruct that healing through a misconceived notion of prayer. The sign from heaven in Jacob 7 not only forced Sherem to the ground, but in some ways recommitted Jacob to the earth as well by driving him to his knees. In the end, the very posture Latter-day Saints use in private prayer may become a way of acknowledging our place and responsibility on earth as much as it is about limiting distraction or communicating humility. We kneel and bow, craning ourselves closer to the earth from which we were formed, accepting our role as God's servants on earth to overcome the world's distance from heaven. In a prayer absent anxieties about our sinful will, we may be better positioned to accomplish the unity of heaven and earth anticipated in the very prayer that echoes throughout Jacob 7: "thy kingdom come" (Matthew 6:10).

Divine Dream Time: The Hope and Hazard of Revelation

Jacob Rennaker

JACOB'S CONCLUDING WORDS ARE AMONG THE MOST POIGNANT in all of scripture: "the time passed away with us, and also our lives passed away like as it were unto us a dream" (Jacob 7:26). However, far from being the mere poetic waxing of a dying man, I believe that the concept of "dreams" is critical to understanding Jacob's theology and his writings as a whole. Within our dreams, we experience time differently than when we are awake. Rather than events following after each other in a linear and understandable way, they often present a different sort of logic altogether—one where time is not linear and connections between events are mysterious at best. Jacob's description of revelation seems to reflect this sort of "dream time."[1] In fact, Jacob's father, Lehi, explicitly describes one of his own revelations as dreamlike: "Behold, I have dreamed a dream, or in other words, I have seen a vision" (1 Nephi 8:2).[2] In my view, Jacob 7 highlights the dreamlike nature of revelatory

---

1. Canonically speaking, Nephi's vision (1 Nephi 11–14) of Lehi's dream/vision (1 Nephi 8) is a good, proximate example of how an individual's experience of divine communication can be both temporally jarring and logically disconnected.

2. I have used Royal Skousen's *The Book of Mormon: The Earliest Text* (New Haven: Yale University Press, 2009) as my base text for Book of Mormon quotations; all emphasis has been added.

experiences, illustrates the dangers inherent in receiving a revelation of God, and demonstrates how to avoid these potential hazards through a "hope in Christ" (Jacob 2:19).

Isn't it about time?

Central to Jacob's perception of the world is his revelatory experience with Christ. Dietrich Bonhoeffer once wrote a letter puzzling over whether or not it is possible to have what he calls a "religionless Christianity."[3] In this letter, he wrestles with the relationship between the structural aspects of "religion" on the one hand and the essence of Christianity on the other, and he investigates how necessarily entangled those two ideas are. Ultimately, Bonhoeffer suggests that there *could* be a form of Christianity that is not bounded by the traditional strictures of religion. In Jacob 7, Sherem seems to be doing just the opposite—he has wrestled with the relationship between the structural aspects of the law of Moses and the essence of Jacob's Christian message and determines that they have been unnecessarily entangled in the public mind. He contends that there should be a form of Nephite religion—completely circumscribed by the law of Moses—that is *not* tied to the idea of Christianity. Instead of a religionless Christianity, Sherem argues for a Christless religiosity among the Nephites.

The conflict between Jacob and Sherem revolves not only around their acceptance of Christ but also around their understanding of time. Sherem begins the story with a very linear way of looking at time and life that is largely oriented toward the past—his knowledge is rooted

---

3. In a letter to Eberhard Bethge, 30 April 1944, Bonhoeffer wrote, "Our entire nineteen hundred years of Christian preaching and theology are built on the 'religious a priori' in human beings. 'Christianity' has always been a form (perhaps the true form) of 'religion.' Yet if it becomes obvious one day that this 'a priori' doesn't exist, that it has been a historically conditioned and transitory form of human expression, then people really will become radically religionless. . . . If religion is only the garb in which Christianity is clothed—and this garb has looked very different in different ages—what then is religionless Christianity?" See Dietrich Bonhoeffer, *Letters and Papers from Prison*, ed. John W. de Gruchy, trans. Isabel Best et al. (Minneapolis: Augsburg Fortress, 2009), 362–63.

squarely in the law of Moses that he so vigorously defends (Jacob 7:7). Sherem is clearly invested in this law and sees it as the necessary foundation of Nephite religion—his way of knowing the right way is focused on the past, through the clearly defined, linear terms outlined in the law of Moses. Sherem's problem with Jacob doesn't appear to be centered in the general concept of Christ's atonement. Rather, he seems much more concerned with Jacob putting so much rhetorical and theological weight on an event that will supposedly happen "many hundred years hence." This is "blasphemy, for no man knoweth of such things; for he cannot tell of things to come" (v. 7). Eschewing the future as unknowable, Sherem is focused on the permanence of the past, where events are fixed in a dependable linear chain that inevitably leads to the present.

At first Jacob seems to express a view that is the polar opposite of Sherem's, a view that is oriented toward the future. And, in a sense, this is correct: Jacob testifies that Christ will come and make an atonement at some unspecified point in the future. However, Jacob's Christ-centered religiosity does not simply require people to change their orientation from looking backward in time to looking forward in time. More is required. A Christ-centered religiosity requires people to step outside the tyranny of linear time and into a dreamlike space. In this dream space, the focus is not on permanence but on possibility. This sort of nonlinear, atemporal Christian framework gives Jacob the ability to see the past *in light of* the future, while still allowing for the mystery of God in the present.

Jacob describes his own particular dreamlike way of experiencing time and life as a "hope in Christ."[4] Jacob first uses this phrase in his sermon to the Nephites at the temple (Jacob 2:19) and then expands on this idea in Jacob 4. In this passage, he states that he "knew of Christo, ... [having] a hope of his glory many hundred years before his coming," and suggests it was this hope in Christ that allowed him to perceive that same hope in "all the holy prophets which were before us"

---

4. For a discussion of the inseparable connection between *hope* and *daydreaming*, see Ernst Bloch, *The Principle of Hope*, trans. Neville Plaice, Stephen Plaice, and Paul Knight (Cambridge, MA: MIT Press, 1986), 77–113.

(Jacob 4:4). This hope in Christ served as an interpretive lens through which Jacob could enter into a qualitatively different relationship with the scriptures. In other words, this "hope" allowed Jacob to experience the words of the prophets not as permanently fixed statements trapped within a linear stream of time but as words suggesting expansive and redemptive possibilities. This also fits with Jacob's statement in chapter 7 that "none of the prophets have written nor prophesied save they have spoken concerning this Christ" (Jacob 7:11). On their surface, the prophetic writings of the Hebrew Bible appear to largely lack explicit references to Jesus Christ. But Jacob's atemporal "hope in Christ" allows him to see clearly the *implicit* Christian dimension of those very same ancient words. And, as one of Sherem's central concerns is with Jacob's "perversion" of the law of Moses (see Jacob 7:7), Jacob also suggests that it was his hope in Christ that allowed him to read even the law in terms of its redemptive possibilities: "For this intent we keep the law of Moses, it pointing our souls to [Christ]. And for this cause it is sanctified unto us for righteousness" (Jacob 4:5).

This reconfiguration of prophetic and legal words from the past and their relationship to Jacob in the present also extends into the future by virtue of his continued hope in Christ. In chapter 4, Jacob again posits a present reconciliation with God through the future atonement of Christ—what he calls a "good hope of glory in [Christ] before he manifesteth himself in the flesh" (Jacob 4:11). Jacob then explains that he received this significant knowledge of the present (in light of the future) through the divine intervention of the Spirit: "For the Spirit speaketh the truth and lieth not. Wherefore it speaketh of things as they really are and of things as they really will be" (Jacob 4:13).[5]

Sherem, because of his own fixed, linear view of time, seems to misunderstand Jacob's worldview because it is centered in a hope in Christ. Jacob's prophecies do not isolate him in a projected future; they secure him firmly to the present. Once he has rooted himself in the

---

5. This particular phrase differs in an interesting way from a similar phrase in the Doctrine and Covenants: "And truth is knowledge of things as they are, and as they were, and as they are to come" (93:24). Perhaps Jacob does not speak here of the Spirit's ability to communicate the truth of the past because he has already covered this subject earlier in the chapter when he discussed the law and the prophets (Jacob 4:4–5).

presence of Christ, Jacob can then perceive truths in both the past and the future. We see this "presentness" of Jacob as he opens his response to Sherem's accusations: "Behold, the Lord God poured in his Spirit into my soul" (Jacob 7:8). This pouring of God's Spirit suggests a present and immediate experience. The phrase is reminiscent of several passages in the Hebrew Bible, of which the book of Joel is a good example: "I will *pour out* my spirit upon all flesh; and your sons and your daughters shall *prophesy*, your old men shall *dream dreams*, your young men shall *see visions*" (Joel 2:28, emphasis added). The Hebrew verb for "pour out" here is שָׁפַךְ (*shaphach*), which means "to pour out, [or] to shed," and "does not mean a gradual pouring . . . but rather a *sudden, massive spillage*."[6] Thus, the phrase "the Lord God poured in his Spirit into my soul" suggests a sudden reception of divine communication that grounds the individual in a revelatory present while opening both the future and the past to a person's understanding.

We can also see this idea of experiencing a divine dream time in Jacob's description of how he received heavenly knowledge. Jacob claims to have seen angels, to have been ministered to by them, and to have heard the Divine voice. Significantly, he frames his account of these experiences with the phrase "from time to time" (Jacob 7:5). The Lord speaking "from time to time" takes Jacob *out* of time and allows him to simultaneously perceive the past (the presence of Christ in the writings of the law and the prophets), the present ("things as they really are"), and the future ("things as they really will be," including Christ's advent in the flesh). Thus, I believe that Jacob's teachings were ultimately focused on becoming open to a temporally charitable hope in Christ. Such teachings helped the people to form a worldview that would allow the Divine to mysteriously and immediately impart knowledge in the present, allowing them to break free of linear time and experience—as Jacob did—the word of the Lord "*from* time [linear time] *to* time [dream time]."

---

6. Ludwig Koehler and Walter Baumgartner, *The Hebrew and Aramaic Lexicon of the Old Testament* (Leiden: Brill, 1994), 1629, s.v. שׁפך, emphasis added.

Jacob's dream and Sherem's nightmare

It appears as though Jacob is able to navigate this dreamlike experience of nonlinear time in a relatively productive way. But Jacob's ability to maintain a coherent framework capable of holding together past, present, and future at the same time was made possible only through his hope in Christ.[7] Jacob's distinctively Christ-centered religiosity created space for this mystery of divine dream time, whereas Sherem's Christ-less religiosity erected barriers God had to overcome in order to reveal that same mystery. To put it another way, Jacob is an open valley into which God can pour his Spirit. Sherem, on the other hand, has erected a dam against God's revelations by focusing entirely on the words of the past (especially as revealed in the law of Moses). Sherem's shattering encounter with God's revelations shows that these revelations can themselves be dangerous if they are forced to overcome human-created barriers.

Perhaps the "power of the Lord" that ultimately comes upon Sherem at the climax of his conflict with Jacob was one of these non-linear, dreamlike experiences that allowed Sherem to truly know about Christ (Jacob 7:15, 17). This view appears to be substantiated by the frenzied shifting references to time in Sherem's confession:

> I *fear* [present] lest I *have committed* [past] the unpardonable sin, for I *have lied* [past] unto God. For I *denied* [past] the Christ and said that I *believed* [past] the scriptures—and they truly *testify* [present] of him. And because that I *have* thus *lied* [past] unto God, I greatly *fear* [present] lest my case *shall be* [future] awful; but I *confess* [present] unto God. (Jacob 7:19)

We can see here the power of the Lord violently breaking Sherem free from the tyranny of linear time and linear thinking—a radical departure from his Christless religiosity that had been oriented primarily

---

7. We can see this principle quite clearly in Alma the Younger's narration of his own "conversion" experience, where the only thing that spares him from the madness of an atemporal revelation (Alma 36:12–16) is his desperate hope in Christ (36:17–20).

toward the past and the heavily sequential nature of the law of Moses. However, this breaking free has a different effect upon Sherem than it does upon Jacob. Sherem doesn't see only the hopeful aspect of the gospel that Jacob has most recently emphasized—the ministering of angels and the word of the Lord. Rather, Sherem is at least equally struck by the nightmarish aspects of this divine dream time. On the one hand, Sherem tells us that through this revelation, he has now experienced "the Christ," "the power of the Holy Ghost," and "the ministering of angels" (Jacob 7:17). Here, three elements are specifically mentioned. But immediately thereafter, we see the other side of this revelation in verse 18. Sherem speaks of hell, of eternity, and of eternal punishment. Once again, three elements are specifically mentioned, but this time, with a much darker tone.

Sherem's problem seems to come from seeing not only the positive and negative repercussions of actions from a nonlinear, dreamlike point of view, but in also trying to fit his past actions *into* this newly acquired atemporal framework. He clearly recognizes both the positive and negative implications of an eternal perspective, but even after experiencing this perspective, he is still oriented toward the past. This is suggested by the language Sherem uses to describe his internal state. He says, "I *fear* lest I have committed the unpardonable sin," not "I *know* that I have committed the unpardonable sin." In other words, Sherem's revelation and his newfound knowledge is not about his definitive condemnation before God nor about his own eternal punishment. He doesn't know these things; he only fears them. But while he recognizes that he has received a knowledge of Christ in the present—Christ is a reality, he really was in the scriptures all along, and he will come "many hundred years" in the future—these revelations are still framed by his own past actions ("I *have lied* unto God").

I would like to suggest that Sherem was not intentionally lying to God or the people with his earlier teachings. I believe that Sherem's anxiety about lying is the result of his wrestle with a new and unfamiliar dream time that has been violently imposed upon him. Sherem is experiencing a sort of revelatory post-traumatic stress syndrome. In these passages, I see Sherem viewing God's revelations from his own personal framework, a framework that unfortunately lacks the sort of charity that a hope in Christ would provide. Sherem is trying to reorganize the pieces of his previously linear worldview, but instead of completely embracing this different way of looking at time and life, Sherem keeps holding on to his previous perspective. In other words, he is trying to force God's new wine into his own old bottles (cf. Matthew 9:17).

In light of his overwhelming revelation of Christ, Sherem is now (understandably) even more sensitive to his past actions that ran counter to Christ. Consider, for instance, his declaration that Jacob was causing the people to "pervert the right way of God" by not keeping the law of Moses (Jacob 7:7) and his claim that "there is no Christ, neither hath been nor never will be" (v. 9). But Sherem still sees each of these past actions as being decisive for his relationship to God, in spite of his newfound knowledge. He has been exposed to a view of Christ's infinite atonement, but he cannot yet allow his own finite mistakes to be swallowed up by that infinite love.

Rather than being condemned by God, Sherem is here condemning himself—and condemning himself needlessly. He sees his past actions as incongruent with his present knowledge, but since time has been shattered for him, both events (his present knowledge of Christ and his past denial of Christ) carry an equal weight in his own judgment. For someone who had been functioning within a strictly linear and temporal framework, the sudden apprehension of a dreamlike, atemporal framework would be maddening (which might help to explain his fixation on eternity and eternal punishment) and could easily lead to Sherem's unnecessarily harsh self-judgment and self-condemnation. In this scenario, God does not strike a person dead after they recognize the error of their ways—Sherem's smiting here may very well be reflexive.[8] Though one could agree with Longfellow that "whom the gods

---

8. We see this very principle at work in Hamlet's famous soliloquy:

> To be, or not to be? That is the question—
> Whether 'tis nobler *in the mind to suffer*
> The slings and arrows of outrageous fortune,
> Or to take arms against a sea of troubles,
> And, by opposing, end them? To die, to sleep—

would destroy, they first make mad,"[9] the text of Jacob nowhere states that God is directly responsible for Sherem's death. A self-inflicted descent into madness, on the other hand, would better explain the fact that in verse 15, Sherem does not die immediately but is "nourished for the space of many days" before he dies. For Sherem, the dreamlike experience of revelation threatens to become a living nightmare.[10]

Jacob, though he clearly understands both the positive and negative aspects of a nonlinear, atemporal framework, does not go mad because of his hope in Christ. In his dreamlike state, Jacob sees Christ not simply as existing in the past (in the words of the prophets—Jacob 7:10–11), the present (the "voice of the Lord" coming to him "from time to time," v. 5) and future (Christ's coming "many hundred years hence," v. 7), but he also understands that Christ's redemption can essentially

---

No more—and by a sleep to say we end
The heartache and the thousand natural shocks
That flesh is heir to—'tis a consummation
Devoutly to be wished! To die, to sleep.
To sleep, perchance to dream—ay, there's the rub,
For in that sleep of death what dreams may come
When we have shuffled off this mortal coil,
Must give us pause. There's the respect
That makes calamity of so long life. (Shakespeare, *Hamlet*, act 3, scene 1, lines 58–71, emphasis added)

9. Henry Wadsworth Longfellow, *The Masque of Pandora* (Boston, MA: James R. Osgood, 1875), 33.

10. There is an interesting connection between dreams, experiencing the Divine, and the possibility of madness at the very outset of the Hebrew Bible. Immediately preceding the creation of the woman, the Lord God causes a "deep sleep to fall upon Adam" (Genesis 2:21). This "deep sleep" (תרדמה, *tardemah*) was translated into Greek using the word ἔκστασις (*ekstasis*), which is related to the English "ecstasy" and "ecstatic." The *Oxford English Dictionary* explains, "The classical senses of ἔκστασις are 'insanity' and 'bewilderment'; but in late Greek the etymological meaning received another application, viz., 'withdrawal of the soul from the body, mystic or prophetic trance'; . . . Both the classical and post-classical senses came into the modern languages, and in the present fig[urative] uses they seem to be blended" (*OED Online*, s.v. "ecstasy, n."). Thus, it is possible to see the "deep sleep" that God set upon Adam as involving some sort of experience with the Divine, which also carried with it the possibility of insanity.

reconfigure the past so that actions once made outside of (and even against) Christ are reconciled to one's present knowledge and experience of grace. Thus, for Jacob, time has not simply been freed from permanence and linearity, but it has also been unified and reconciled in Christ. In other words, both time and life itself have been brought into a special relationship with Christ.

However, this experience of a divine dream time is clearly not all rainbows and unicorns (or cureloms, if you prefer). We see the mental, emotional, and spiritual toll that this sort of nonlinear, atemporal view had on Sherem, and I believe that at the end of Jacob's writings, we see more clearly the sort of toll that even an atemporal view bolstered by a hope in Christ has had on this prophet—he is "lonesome," "solemn," a "wanderer," "hated," and "mourn[ful]" (Jacob 7:26). We can actually see glimpses of the toll that experiencing this divine dream time can cause throughout Jacob's writings—we read of Jacob's "anxiety" (which accounts for exactly half the references to the term *anxiety* in the entire Book of Mormon), his being "weighed down" (Jacob 2:3), his burden (vv. 9, 23), and his "grief" (vv. 6–7, which, incidentally, seems quite similar to the grief of the Lord—appearing a staggering eight times in Jacob's allegory of the olive tree in Jacob 5—suggesting that even God's own dream time can sometimes be painful).

What, then, makes this temporally disorienting, dreamlike experience with the Divine worth the trouble? Perhaps Jacob found hope in his father Lehi's deathbed blessing for him that God would "consecrate thine afflictions for thy gain" (2 Nephi 2:2).[11] Yes, there would be afflictions—perhaps most especially in experiencing time and life "like as it

---

11. Echoes of priestly language in this phrase neatly tie together divine dream time and a hope in Christ. In Leviticus 21:10, the author explains that the high priest had not only been consecrated (literally, "his hand was filled [with sacred oil]"), but that the anointing oil (literally מְשִׁיחַ [*meshiach*] or χριστος [*christos*] oil) had been "poured out upon his head" (my translation). Thus, in "pouring out" his disorienting, dream-inducing Spirit into Jacob's soul (Jacob 7:8), God could at the same time use that oil-like Spirit to anoint the priestly Jacob unto holiness (Jacob 1:18). Such priestly imagery may help to explain the frequent uses of the term Christ in Jacob 7 (nearly half of its uses in the entire book of Jacob), as opposed to other epithets for the Son of God that Nephi seems to prefer in his writings.

were unto . . . a dream" (Jacob 7:26)—but through such an experience in Christ, Jacob could also gain both time *and* life.

A waking dream

If we return to the final verses that Jacob wrote before he died and reread Jacob 7:26 carefully, we see that Jacob seems to be encouraging us to read his religious writings from within a similar dreamlike framework. He states that the Nephite experience of both time and life were *"like as it were* unto us a dream." The consecutive use of the comparative words *like* and *as it were* may be intentionally evoking a dreamlike state. In fact, Jacob's text seems to be structured in a way to bring us, the audience, into this divine dream time. Within this chapter alone, we are confronted with an odd shifting of tenses and strange ways of talking about time: *"now* it *came* to pass," *"from* time *to time,"* "nourished for the *space* of many days," *"before* that I *should* die," "my Father which *was* in heaven," "they *sought* . . . to destroy us *continually,"* "it came to pass that I Jacob *began* to be old," "the time *passed away* with us," and "I *saw* that I *must soon* go down to my grave." Such vacillations in temporal phraseology suggest a nonlinear sense of dreaming, preparing the audience for God to break into their own sense of time and life.[12]

By crafting his text in a way that would help ease his audience into a divine dream time (stabilized by a hope in Christ), Jacob's textual vision resonates strongly with that of the deeply Christian author George MacDonald, who wrote:

---

12.   On a much larger scale, we can see a sort of dream logic organizing the entire book of Jacob in the constant shifting between genres from chapter to chapter—in the first chapter, narrative gives way to the quotation of a public sermon (in chapters 2–3), which is immediately followed by an editorial explanation (chapter 4), which leads directly into an extended allegory about plants (chapter 5), which is followed by an analysis of that allegory (chapter 6) that seems to definitively end his writings (6:13), before beginning a brand new narrative (chapter 7) that officially ends the book with the statement that Jacob's experience of time and life has been like a dream (7:26). It is almost as if Jacob has been inviting us to join him in this divine dream time all along.

> Strange dim memories . . . look out upon me in the broad
> daylight, but I never dream now. It may be, notwith-
> standing, that, when most awake, I am only dreaming
> the more! But when I wake *at last* into that life which, as
> a mother her child, carries this life in its bosom, I shall
> know that I wake, and shall doubt no more. . . . Our life
> is no dream, but it should—and *will* perhaps—become
> one.[13]

Like MacDonald, Jacob ultimately invites his audience into a relationship with Christ—one that can transform their broken lives into a
redemptive, waking dream.

---

13. George MacDonald, *Lilith* (London: Chatto & Windus, 1896), 350–51.

"To Destroy Us Continually": Time and the *Katechon* in Jacob 7

Jeremy Walker

THE GOAL OF THIS PAPER IS TO ENGAGE A SINGLE CHAPTER in the Book of Mormon and take it seriously as a theologically significant and sophisticated work. The motivation is threefold: First, to develop one possible framework for understanding the formal features and narrative movement of the text of Jacob 7; second, to demonstrate that, in contrast to sentiments from Mark Twain[1] and others, the Book of Mormon has a literary and theological richness readily found in the text; and third, to articulate how the Pauline idea of the *katechon* can open a new understanding of messianic time, specifically in how it provides a basis for thinking of soteriology as separate from eschatology. In other words, the idea of the *katechon* can reveal the messianic as a category related to lived experiences of time.

Messianic time

We have inherited from ancient Greek two terms for time: *chronos* and *kairos*. From *chronos* we derive various terms for measurements of time such as chronology or chronometer (e.g., a clock*). Chronos* refers to the sequential passing of measurable time and *kairos* to the proper or right

---

1. See Mark Twain, *Roughing It* (1872; repr., New York: Penguin Books, 1985), 146.

time for something to happen. A rough distinction would be to see *chronos* as quantitative and *kairos* as qualitative. Messianic time takes these two concepts and weaves them together. This weaving is present if not explicit in the philosopher Walter Benjamin's essay "Theses on the Philosophy of History," which generated significant philosophical interest in the notion of messianic time by later philosophers such as Jacques Derrida and Giorgio Agamben. Benjamin argues that "the present . . . as a model of messianic time, comprises the entire history of mankind in an enormous abridgment."[2] For Benjamin, messianic time exists both as a particular moment (*kairos*) and as a capacious account of the passage of time, or in other words, history (*chronos*). As I work through manifestations of messianic time in Jacob 7, it is this weaving of *chronos* and *kairos* that is being invoked: a sense of the moment, the here and now, that is both the right moment and, contained within it, a sense of the passing of time. My invocation of messianic time is not a formulation of a moment disconnected or transcending context and history, but a moment abounding and flourishing in chronological time.

The *katechon*

Another key concept in this paper is the *katechon*. Later in the paper I will more fully delve into its origin in 2 Thessalonians, but by way of summary, *katechon* is a term Paul uses that refers to a force that restrains evil (the antichrist) and prevents the end of the world and the arrival of the Messiah. Since this force restrains the arrival of the antichrist and the end of the world, it also, by extension, restrains the arrival of the Messiah, who is to destroy the antichrist and eradicate evil. The Italian philosopher Roberto Esposito says of the *katechon* that "in delaying the explosion of evil . . . it also at the same time delays the final victory of the principle of good. The triumph of evil is held in check, true, but the divine *parousia* [presence] is also delayed by its

---

2. Walter Benjamin, "Theses on the Philosophy of History," in *Illuminations*, ed. Hannah Arendt, trans. Harry Zohn (New York: Schocken Books, 1969), 263.

very existence. Its function is positive, but negatively so."[3] The concept gained prominence in the work of the political theorist Carl Schmitt, who theorizes that the *katechon* was the driving concept for the Christian empire of the Middle Ages and that "the empire lasted . . . only as long as the idea of the *katechon* was alive."[4] For Schmitt, the reason the Christian empire endured was because of a self-conception of being able to block the arrival of the antichrist. The empire was itself a means to fulfill a sense of Christian responsibility to prevent the horrors accompanying the end of the world.

What is fascinating for my purposes is the way in which Schmitt resituates this term and expands it. It is not that Schmitt necessarily modifies Paul's use of the term but, rather, that he is saying that the understanding derived from its usage in Paul came to have a direct social and political manifestation during the Christian empire. My aim is to do theologically what Schmitt does sociopolitically: to take the use of the term seriously as a component of messianic time and to draw out some of the theological tensions Schmitt overlooks, such as the dynamic of restraining the antichrist that consequently restrains the return of the Messiah. The messianic can be and often is thought of as a component of the present moment, of the now, as somehow part of lived experience and not simply as a figure of the past or the future. The *katechon*, this restraining force, is clearly linked to both the messianic and to the end of the world. However, in my view, the term is too readily linked *primarily* to the end of the world (i.e., the *eschaton*) and only *secondarily* to the messianic as such. What Jacob 7 offers is a way to see how the *katechon* might be linked primarily to the messianic *present* and only secondarily to the end of the world. This would mean that the *katechon* could be viewed as a component of lived experience and not only as a part of the Christian view of the end of the world.

3. Roberto Esposito, *Immunitas: The Protection and Negation of Life,* trans. Zakiya Hanafi (Cambridge: Polity Press, 2011), 63.
4. Carl Schmitt, *The Nomos of the Earth in the International Law of Jus Publicum Europaeum,* trans. G. L. Ulmen (New York: Telos Press, 2006), 60.

"To destroy continually"

Near the end of Jacob, chapter 7, Jacob uses a provocative phrase as he reports his people's failure in "restor[ing] the Lamanites to the knowledge of the truth."[5] He comments: "And [the Lamanites] sought by the power of their arms to destroy us continually" (Jacob 7:24). The grammar here does something fascinating, and it is this moment that led me to explore the various ways in which this text relates to messianic time.

The key phrase here is "to destroy us continually." The phrase opens up multiple, equally possible readings that pivot on the term *continually*, which is doing some heavy lifting semantically. Without the terminal adverb, the sentence sensibly reads, "and they sought by the power of their arms to destroy us." But adding the adverb *continually* changes the meaning of the entire sentence and adds a level of paradox. What would it mean to seek to "destroy continually"? Is Jacob saying that his people were destroyed or not destroyed? It would be easy to sidestep this provocative moment by deciding that the adverb *continually* modifies the seeking of the Lamanites, that they "sought continually" to destroy Jacob's people. However, I think there is good reason to read this sentence, instead, as a paradox and ask how someone could have a goal to do something that by definition can never be (entirely) done.

Certainly, we could also read this sentence as indicating an ongoing attempt to kill individual Nephites, but doing so elides the potency of the actual language. "To destroy continually" is a paradoxical phrase and foregrounds a logic that, on my reading, is crucial for parsing out the messianic texture of the chapter. To destroy continually is to never (entirely) destroy. To continue destroying means you will always be locked in an act you can never quite complete but, nonetheless, continually attempt. The logic, here, is that in order to *continually* destroy, you can never entirely destroy *and* never cease the work of destruction. As I examined Jacob 7's formal features and narrative movements,

---

5. I have used Royal Skousen's *The Book of Mormon: The Earliest Text* (New Haven: Yale University Press, 2009) as my base text for Book of Mormon quotations; any emphasis has been added.

I began to see this paradoxical phrase as a distillation of the chapter's explicit engagement with messianic time.

In my view, Jacob 7 is significant as a messianic text because it opens a way to retheorize the role of the *katechon* in the experience of messianic *parousia* [presence]. It uncouples soteriology (the study of salvation) from eschatology (the study of the end of the world). It suggests a form of salvation available now in lived experience, a form of salvation that is recursive rather than linear and that, as a result, is capable of immediately addressing the vicissitudes of human experience. The problem with models of soteriology that tightly tie soteriology to eschatology is that even if the experience of *parousia* matters in some way now, it really only matters *now* because it will matter in the future. Jacob 7 may offer a way to bring the messiah into the *now* of our lived experience rather than postponing that redemption for a future day at the world's end. On my reading, Jacob 7 is not an eschatological text, it is a katechological text. And, as a result, it is most certainly a messianic text.

The apostle Paul and the *katechon*

Before discussing Jacob 7, I want to take some time to unpack the idea of the *katechon* and messianic time. In 2 Thessalonians 2: 3–8, Paul articulates a type of relationship between the messiah, the lawless one (often understood as an antichrist figure), the end of time, and the force that restrains the lawless one. As rendered by Giorgio Agamben, the key passage reads:

> Let no one deceive you in any way; for that day will not come unless there come a falling away [*apostasia*] first and the lawless one be revealed, the one destined for destruction He opposes and exalts himself above every so-called god or object of worship, so that he takes his seat in the temple of God, declaring himself to be God. Do you not remember that I told you these things when I was still with you? And you know what is now restraining [*katechon*] him, so that he may be revealed

when his time comes. For the mystery of lawlessness is already at work, but only until the one who now restrains [*katechōn*] it is removed. And then the lawless one will be revealed, whom the Lord Jesus will destroy with the breath of his mouth, annihilating him by the manifestation of his coming.[6]

In this passage Paul tells us that before the end of all things, the "lawless one" must be revealed. Then, after he is revealed, Christ will appear and destroy him. This "lawless one" can be understood as an antichrist—or even *the* antichrist John discusses in 1 John 2:18—though there is nothing in the text describing this lawless one as an antichrist explicitly. I should pause to highlight two points here where 2 Thessalonians intersects with Jacob 7: Both texts feature a figure often termed *antichrist*, even though the text does not name them as such, and both texts deal with the issue of messianic arrival.

Second Thessalonians 2 is typically read as discussing the second coming of Christ and addresses the question: Why has Jesus not returned? What in the world is holding him back? In response, Paul tells us that before Jesus can return, the "lawless one" must be revealed. However, in verses 6 and 7, he also repeats that there is someone or something restraining the lawless one. This thing that restrains the lawless one must get out of the way in order for the lawless one to be revealed, and only then will Christ appear and annihilate the "lawless one."

This provocative figure of the force that restrains the lawless one has ignited fascination not only among theologians but among political philosophers as well. The Greek term for this force described as restraining or holding back the lawless one is *katechon*. The *katechon* has captured philosophers' imaginations, in part because of the strange way that it operates: in holding back the lawless one (often understood to be Satan or evil), the *katechon*, this restraining force,

---

6. Second Thessalonians 2:3–8, as translated in Giorgio Agamben, *The Time That Remains: A Commentary on the Letter to the Romans*, trans. Patricia Dailey (Stanford: Stanford University Press, 2005), 109.

is also ironically holding back the arrival of the messiah. The French philosopher Peter Szendy concisely articulates this dynamic when he says: "Withholding the coming of an Antichrist who in his turn precedes the coming of the Messiah, the *katechon* amounts to a kind of postponement of a postponement."[7] How should we understand this force that both holds evil in abeyance but also prevents its annihilation?

Agamben, messianic time, and the *katechon*

In his book *The Time That Remains*, Giorgio Agamben analyzes the first verse of Paul's letter to the Romans and argues that the "first ten words recapitulate the meaning of the text in its entirety."[8] The meaning of the text he seeks to foreground is the messianic significance in the phrase *ho nyn kairos* from Romans 8. Agamben translates this phrase as "the time of the now."[9] Agamben's argument essentially turns on explicating what this "now" means. He asks, "What does it mean to live in the Messiah, and what is the messianic life? What is the structure of messianic time?"[10] He answers those questions by digging into this "now."

For Agamben, the time of the "now" relates to how "the messianic—the ungraspable quality of the 'now'—is the very opening through which we may seize hold of time, achieving our representation of time, making it end."[11] Through this ungraspable "now" we are able to grasp a messianic presence and glimpse a different order of time. Agamben formulates this as a sort of paradox:

> The Messiah has already arrived, the messianic event has already happened, but its presence contains within itself another time, which stretches its *parousia* [presence],

7. Peter Szendy, "Katechon," in *Political Concepts: A Critical Lexicon*, ed. J. M. Bernstein, Adi Ophir, and Ann Laura Stoler, accessed September 1, 2017, http://www.politicalconcepts.org/katechon-peter-szendy/.
8. Agamben, *Time That Remains*, 6.
9. Agamben, *Time That Remains*, 2.
10. Agamben, *Time That Remains*, 18.
11. Agamben, *Time That Remains*, 100.

not in order to defer it, but, on the contrary, to make it graspable. For this reason, each instant may be, to use Benjamin's words, the "small door through which the Messiah enters." The Messiah always already had his time, meaning he simultaneously makes time his and brings it to fulfillment.[12]

Agamben gives a couple examples of this messianic time, one of which is a description of the experience of faith. He says:

> What then is the world of faith? Not a world of substance and qualities, not a world in which the grass is green, the sun is warm, and the snow is white. No, it is not a world of predicates, of existences and of essences, but a world of indivisible events, in which I do not judge, nor do I believe that the snow is white and the sun is warm, but I am transported and displaced in the snow's-being-white and in the sun's-being-warm. In the end, it is a world in which I do not believe that Jesus, such-and-such a man, is the Messiah, only-begotten son of God, begotten and not created, consubstantial in the Father. I only believe in Jesus Messiah; I am carried away and enraptured in him, in such a way that "I do not live, but the Messiah lives in me" (Gal. 2:20).[13]

This experience of faith is the experience of messianic *parousia*. Messianic time transforms chronological time, but it also transforms reasoned experience. It is not simply "being in the moment" but rather being *through* a moment, a moment in which being enraptured is not due to a matrix of reasons to be enraptured but to an experience of the messiah that then reaches outward. Just as the now is the small door through which the messiah enters and transforms chronological time without erasing it, the experience of the messiah transforms experience

---

12. Agamben, *Time That Remains*, 71.
13. Agamben, *Time That Remains*, 129.

without erasing it. The messianic is not substitutional but additive, and it is this addition that then transforms. It is not simply a new thing replacing the old thing, but a transformation of the old in a way that retains the old in the new. We see this in the imagery of dying in the Messiah to live again in Romans 6. It is not death as an end—which would simply be replacing the old with the new—but rather death as a new life that retains something of the old as well.

It is during this book-length elaboration on the messianic "time of the now" that Agamben briefly engages the figure of the *katechon*. Agamben's formulation of the "now" of messianic time is incredibly provocative and sustained, but his engagement with the *katechon* moves too quickly. Agamben summarizes the significance of the *katechon* by saying:

> The *katechōn* is therefore the force—the Roman Empire as well as every constituted authority—that clashes with and hides *katargēsis* [inoperativity/weakness], the state of tendential lawlessness that characterizes the messianic and in this sense delays unveiling the "mystery of lawlessness." The unveiling of this mystery entails bringing to light the inoperativity of the law and the substantial illegitimacy of each and every power in messianic time.[14]

This reading of the *katechon* strictly within its context in 2 Thessalonians is useful and generative. But it is also slightly constraining and does not fully account for the mechanism of the *katechon* because it is primarily focused on the political rather than on the theological aspects.

The *katechon*, as Agamben states, delays the unveiling of lawlessness, but in this moment Agamben could too easily be read as conflating the dual operation of the *katechon*. This restraining force prevents the lawlessness of evil as well as the lawlessness of the messianic. It prevents both the destructive aspect of transformation as well as the generative aspect. One of the potential pitfalls when thinking about

---

14. Agamben, *Time That Remains*, 111.

the *katechon* is that it is already such a rich idea in its eschatological or political context as a force that restrains evil and simultaneously blocks the triumph of overturning evil. It is this richness that can prevent us from seeing the breadth of the term in a theological, messianic context of the time of the now.

The term is more than a mere step on the ladder of eschatology; it foregrounds the experience of *parousia* of the messiah by situating the messianic in a soteriologically recursive rather than a soteriologically teleological context. To think of the messianic as a soteriologically recursive event would mean that, just as the experience of messianic time can ebb and flow for an individual, so too does the *katechon* operate as an oscillating force that restrains both evil and salvation while *also* being the very mechanism by which the messianic manifests itself in the present moment. Thinking about the messianic only in terms of a linear eschatology limits the way the messianic operates as a component of lived religious experience. In my view, this lived experience of the katechonic paradox of the messianic reverberates in Jacob 7 in multiple registers, in particular in that provocative phrase with which I began: "to destroy us continually."

The continual *katechon*

In my reading, "to destroy us continually" precisely captures the figure of the *katechon*: it seeks to accomplish something but can never quite complete the task while continuing to exist itself. The *katechon* must restrain evil but never destroy it. The *katechon* in Paul restrains evil, but in the act of restraining it, it prevents the arrival of the messianic return that would end evil. It tries to stop evil but can never fully end it. In other words, the *katechon* must destroy continually: it must fight against something that it must *continually* fight and can never stop fighting. Implicit in this *katechonic* logic of destroying continually is the sense of restraint and holding back. The work of destruction would be completed if some force were not blocking it and holding it in abeyance. It is important to remember that often in Christian theology the second coming of the messiah is marked by destruction, and the *katechon* is holding that destruction back. It is impossible to think of the second coming and the restraining force of 2 Thessalonians without also invoking some notion of destruction or threat.

This phrase "to destroy continually" is also evocative of a related phrase from the French philosopher Maurice Blanchot, one that Agamben finds fascinating, even though he mistakenly conflates two different phrases in Blanchot due to their conceptual similarity.[15] In *The Infinite Conversation*, Blanchot, in discussing Robert Antelme's writings of his experience during the Holocaust, remarks:

> Through reading such a book we begin to understand that *man is indestructible and that he can nonetheless be destroyed.* This happens in affliction. In affliction we approach the limit where, deprived of the power to say 'I,' deprived also of the world, we would be nothing other than this Other that we are not.[16]

In *The Writing of the Disaster*, Blanchot also engages the effects of affliction, and again he comments on this issue of destruction and the human when he states:

> Human weakness, which even affliction does not divulge, penetrates us on account of our belonging at every instant to the immemorial past of our death—on account of *our being indestructible because always and infinitely destroyed.*[17]

In each statement Blanchot figures the human—and even more intimately in the second passage as "us"—as both indestructible yet still something that can be destroyed. I'm sure it's already obvious that there is clear overlap between "infinitely destroyed" and "destroyed

---

15. See Lisa Guenther, "Resisting Agamben: The Biopolitics of Shame and Humiliation," *Philosophy and Social Criticism* 38/1 (2012): 19n12.

16. Maurice Blanchot, *The Infinite Conversation*, trans. Susan Hanson (Minneapolis: University of Minnesota Press, 1993), 130, emphasis added.

17. Maurice Blanchot, *The Writing of the Disaster*, trans. Ann Smock (Lincoln: University of Nebraska Press, 1995), 30, emphasis added.

continually." In each case the issue is about something that endures, and even though for Blanchot this understanding of infinite destruction and indestructibility emerge in the context of a severely dehumanizing experience of torture and affliction, a messianic gesture lurks in his formulation. Even in a being who is tortured and afflicted, even in that extremity, there is something that remains, something crucial that cannot be fully destroyed.

Commenting on Blanchot's statement about infinite destruction, Agamben states that "if man is that which may be infinitely destroyed, this also means that something other than this destruction, and within this destruction, remains, and that man is this remnant."[18] He then goes on to say that, in Paul "the remnant no longer consists in a concept turned toward the future, as with the prophets; it concerns a present experience that defines the messianic 'now.'"[19] Just as Agamben sees a commentary on the messianic in Blanchot related to Paul's thinking, so too do I see this form of messianic thinking present in Jacob's words in Jacob 7. In my view, this notion of infinite or continual destruction is even more transparent in Jacob 7 because of the text's juxtaposition of a divine presence that is experienced communally with the experience of constant threat and affliction. In light of the katechon, Jacob is not simply making a jarring leap from the experience of divine manifestation in his encounter with Sherem (see Jacob 7:21–23) to the brief history he provides about the devastation of war (see Jacob 7:24): He is drawing on a lived experience of messianic time that can operate even in these awful moments.

Looking forward backwardly

Let's jump to the future and move backward. It can be helpful to shift forward in the Book of Mormon to see the culmination of this messianic theology that is at play in Jacob 7. Jacob's grandson, Jarom, hundreds of years before Christ's appearance, articulates this messianic theology straightforwardly:

---

18. Agamben, *Time That Remains*, 53.
19. Agamben, *Time That Remains*, 55.

> Wherefore the prophets and the priests and the teach-
> ers did labor diligently, . . . teaching the law of Moses
> and the intent for which it was given, persuading them
> to *look forward* unto the Messiah and believe in him *to*
> *come* as though he *already was.* (Jarom 1:11)

Notice the odd temporality here that constitutes a sort of paradox. The people are taught to "look forward" on the one hand and, on the other hand, to also believe in the messiah "as though he already was." They look forward as if they were looking backward. They look forward backwardly. Not only is this passage provocative in its presentation of a mode of temporality that looks forward backwardly, but the potency of the "as though" phrase highlights the paradox of the formulation "already was."

In this passage, the method of looking forward to a messiah is accomplished through a way of looking "as though" or "as if." This conditional mode of perception is not just pretense. It is not false. Rather it is a mode of perception that stabilizes and imbues with meaning. In the nineteenth-century philosopher of science Hans Vaihinger's discussion of the "as if" of reality, Vaihinger argues that this "as if" mode is crucial both to scientific reasoning (as with a model of an atom that gestures toward the structure of an atom but is itself a fiction) and to perception in everyday experience (and, as Agamben points out, this "as if" is crucial to language itself).[20] I think Vaihinger goes too far in framing the "as if" as only an accepted falsity to aid perception, but his observation is astute all the same. It at least pushes us in the right direction in thinking about how this kind of "as if" reasoning may be at work in Jarom 1:11.

It is critical to recognize that Jarom is not advocating that his people embrace something that is false or that they live according to something that is outside reality. Quite the opposite. Jarom is urging his people to live in a way that incorporates the advent of the messiah

---

20. See Hans Vaihinger, *The Philosophy of "As If"*: *A System of the Theoretical, Practical and Religious Fictions of Mankind*, trans. C. K. Ogden (London: Routledge and Kegen, 1935), 15, 17; and Agamben, *Time That Remains*, 35.

through an "as if" that is not mere fantasy but, instead, is the manifestation of an anticipated future in the present. This is different than a platitude like "live as if each day is your last" or "dance as if no one is watching." Those platitudes are about a specific mindset that dodges conditions of lived experience or reality. They are about embracing an idea that one doesn't believe to be true but still provides a sort of ad hoc motivation.

In Jarom, on the contrary, the temporality of the "as if" is about acting not on something that is outside reality, but acting on something that is based on a future event. This posture is foundational, for example, to forms of political or social activism that perceive a future world in such a way that their present actions follow from that future not as a fiction but as an expectation. It is a question of acting in the present in light of a future event toward which one had been looking. It is looking forward backwardly and living in a new present, a present that is more than the present, a present that, through this "as if" mechanism, displaces itself, meaning that this "new" present is not somehow casting some "old" present out. The new present is not simply displacing an old present because this messianic present, this time of the now, is both itself and something more. When the messiah enters time in someone's experience, the person remains where they are physically, by a tree or in a grocery store or in a church. But that place, that present, becomes more capacious than it would have been otherwise. We are dealing with a shift in the perception of temporality that moves beyond fantasy. This mode of thinking is broader than fictionalism as articulated by Vaihinger. While my approach would include a concept like strategic essentialism, it also departs from these ideas by incorporating more indeterminacy in terms of the questions of falsity. For example, when people invest in retirement accounts or buy groceries for the end of the week, they are operating "as if" those things were operationally true but not based on a recognized falsity. I want to mark a distinction between the "as if" that operates based on a known falsity and an "as if" that operates on a sort of indeterminacy. It is the latter that is relevant for this paper.

Jacob 7 and the messianic

This structure of looking forward backwardly in Jarom 1:11 can be traced back to Jacob 7—from Jarom the grandson to Jacob his grandfather—and this similarity is especially evident, I think, in the chapter's structure. My purpose in laying out some of the key features of Jacob 7, therefore, is to develop an answer to the question of how looking forward backwardly is possible. I want to work through three features of Jacob 7 that gesture toward messianic time and the *katechon*: (1) Jacob 7's place in the narrative dynamics of the small plates, (2) the way the summary at the beginning of the book of Jacob unequally summarizes the contents of the book by focusing on increasingly smaller portions of the text, and (3), most significantly, how Jacob 7 features a dynamic I'm calling messianic oscillation, a dynamic in which something that happens in one verse is undone in the next. These features individually and collectively foreground a robust messianic theology at work in the text.

The place of Jacob 7 in the broader context of the small plates is striking for two reasons: (1) we encounter the first named character in the New World after the exodus of Lehi and his family, and (2) we encounter a return of narrative after a heavy pause in the text through much of 2 Nephi and Jacob. To start out, Sherem is the first newly named character in the promised land. Jacob (who authors the book of Jacob) and his brother Joseph were previously the last named characters, and they are mentioned on the ship before arriving in the new land in 1 Nephi 18. For ninety-one pages we are not introduced to any new characters—until Jacob 7 when we meet Sherem. In this respect, Jacob 7 stands out from the preceding chapters. In a way, it announces the rush of the subsequent chapters that are saturated with the introduction of new characters.

The second reason the chapter is striking, which is related to the first, is that it marks a return to narrative. A key way the Book of Mormon tracks narrative is through its use of the phrase "it came to pass." Certainly the phrase can be redundant, but it is also useful as an indicator of genre distinctions since strictly sermonic texts do not feature the phrase. If we set aside the lengthy sections of cited text that Nephi and Jacob include, the phrase "it came to pass" occurs approximately four times per page in 1 Nephi. But in 2 Nephi and Jacob, it occurs, on average, only on every other page. The phrase thus occurs eight times more frequently in 1 Nephi than in 2 Nephi and Jacob combined. That difference is even more striking when we recognize that 1 Nephi is fifty-three pages long, while 2 Nephi and Jacob combined are eighty-two pages. This indicates that 1 Nephi features more narrative than 2 Nephi and Jacob. Narratively speaking, these groupings do reflect a significant division. However, Jacob 7 marks the full-fledged return of narrative to the small plates. It marks a narrative return to presence, to temporality that can be experienced through narrative.

If we assume that Jacob authored the introductory heading to his own book, then Jacob establishes yet another messianic peculiarity in the way he prioritizes chapter 7 in his introduction to the book as a whole. This introductory heading reads as follows: "The words of his preaching unto his brethren. He confoundeth a man who seeketh to overthrow the doctrine of Christ. A few words concerning the history of the people of Nephi." These three descriptive phrases, following the convention of Nephi's introduction (a convention we see carried out throughout the Book of Mormon), summarize the text sequentially as follows:

1. "The words of his preaching unto his brethren" (refers to Jacob 1–6)
2. "He confoundeth a man who seeketh to overthrow the doctrine of Christ" (refers to Jacob 7:1–23)
3. "A few words concerning the history of the people of Nephi" (refers to Jacob 7:24–27)

Each descriptive phrase progressively summarizes a smaller scope of the material. Where the first covers six whole chapters, the second covers just twenty-three verses from a single chapter, and the last only four verses from a single chapter. We see here not just a bizarre method of summary where each descriptive phrase accounts for an increasingly smaller portion of the text, but also an emphasis on the significance of each section to Jacob personally. Jacob is drawing our attention toward the final chapter of his book.

In my view, this summary suggests a messianic component where the moment of messianic presence transforms time in such a way that the "now" may seem ephemeral and only significant as part of a greater whole but actually contains significance in itself that is not dependent on the whole. The fact that the third descriptive phrase covers only four verses while the first covers six chapters enacts the way messianic presence inhabits time: These two "moments," these two descriptive phrases from the summary, are similar in form. Both are short, but the disparity in the amount of content summarized signals that the final four verses of the text, Jacob 7:24–27, hold a greater degree of importance. While covering a huge span of years, the text of Jacob 7 itself contracts. It dilates in chronological time and contracts in kairotic time. In this sense, the introductory heading's strange summary is not simply about content. The heading could instead alert us to the kind of messianic temporality in play in Jacob 7 by *performing* a messianic contraction of time. It is this contraction that I now want to address in earnest.

Messianic oscillation: Part one

The movement of the narrative in Jacob 7 is from instability to stability and back to instability again. The text puts this dynamic in play when Jacob 7 introduces the character of Sherem, a man who is said to be quite intelligent and a highly proficient orator (Jacob 7:4). He is also, Jacob tells us, a liar who is trying to persuade the Nephite people to reject their religious traditions and beliefs (Jacob 7:2). This man Sherem is a disruptive force. People begin to follow him. He flatters them (Jacob 7:2). He causes dissension (Jacob 7:3). Through him, a condition of instability emerges. With Sherem's arrival, a potential shift in the social order becomes possible.

It is in these circumstances that Sherem and Jacob encounter one another. A lot is riding on this encounter. If Jacob cannot refute Sherem's argument, then a radical shift in the composition of Nephite society will result. Why are the stakes so high? Because as a consecrated priest and teacher over the people (see 2 Nephi 5:26) and brother to the now deceased founder of their society, Jacob is viewed as the spiritual leader of the people and Sherem's influence on the people is starting to attenuate Jacob's authority. There would have been no need for the people to experience a renewed sense of religious devotion in Jacob 7:23 unless they had become less devout and therefore less influenced by Jacob. Everything Jacob's brother Nephi had built, and everything that Jacob himself maintained, was based on their belief in a messiah. It is the reason for the schism in Lehi's family, a schism that resulted in wars. This belief in a messiah is a foundational feature of their communal identity. If Sherem can displace it, then things will never be the same. And Jacob knows it. Miraculously, God strikes Sherem down after he seeks a sign (Jacob 7:13, 15). Sherem then admits his wrongdoing (v. 17), and the people of Nephi have a powerful experience that leads to a time of peace (v. 23).

By all accounts, this is a story of triumph. The seemingly evil usurper Sherem attempts to cause a radical shift in belief among the people, but he fails, disaster is averted, and the people come together even more unified than before, even more convinced in their belief in a messiah. One would think Jacob would be celebrating. He did it! He won! However, this story of triumph only precedes Jacob's final and strikingly melancholic words. Immediately after describing his great success, Jacob recounts their subsequent inability to sway their enemies (the people of his elder brothers), the Lamanites. The story of triumph is turned on its head, and the chapter ends by mentioning not only their failure with the Lamanites but Jacob's detailed account of his own depressed state of mind.

> I conclude this record . . . by saying that the time passed away with us, and also our lives passed away like as it were unto us a dream, we being a lonesome and a solemn people, wanderers cast out from Jerusalem, born in tribulation in a wild wilderness, and hated of our brethren, which caused wars and contentions; wherefore we did mourn out our days. (Jacob 7:26)

This dynamic raises the question: Why would Jacob recount this narrative of triumph only to then undo it in the final four verses? I want to suggest that the text is not simply undoing the narrative of triumph but that, instead, it is crafting an argument about messianic presence. If this narrative of Jacob 7 were to follow a teleological arc of salvation, then Sherem would operate either as a Satan/Judas figure preventing the arrival of salvation or as the Christ figure through whom salvation arrives. Alternatively, Jacob could be seen as a messiah figure trampling on evil ideas and bringing salvation to the people. But that is not Jacob's move here. Jacob does not attempt to typologically overlay his experience with Sherem with a grand narrative of salvation. Instead, Jacob presents a narrative of salvation that is experientially tenuous. He wins, but only partially and not for long. This does not undermine the profound significance of his triumph over Sherem, but it does recontextualize the story. It suggests that the messianic does not simply operate on a model of linear temporality.

When Jacob says in 7:26 that "time passed away with us," he suggests a model of time that is not simply chronological. "Passed away" is a common phrase in the Book of Mormon to refer to the passage of time. But here Jacob complicates that usage. In this instance, time does more than pass away, it passes away "with us." Rather than the people being "in" time, time passes away "with" them. And this kind of time is experiential. It has to do with time as it is lived. It has to do with how their "lives passed away"—just like time (Jacob 7:26).

The final reference to time in Jacob 7:26—the people did "mourn out their days"—is similarly peculiar. They do not mourn "throughout" their days. Rather, they mourn "out" their time. Jacob is not providing a straightforward historical account; he is describing a lived experience of time that is about movement and fulfillment. Their time, their days, are "with them," and those days are something that they can "mourn out." In my view, these constructions are potent gestures toward messianic time and the mechanism of its fulfillment, the *katechon*. Time in this passage leaves, remains with, and is something that can be accomplished. It leaves when time "passes away," it remains when it is described as "with us," and it is accomplished when those "days" can be mourned out in the same way that an idea could be worked out. Time becomes the object being mourned. This is, effectively, a moment where the *katechon* has been removed and the evil or negativity it restrained pours in. This moment of mourning is the moment that passes before the messiah enters into the present and reshapes temporality.

When Jacob describes his interaction with Sherem, Jacob effectively functions as a *katechon*. He makes every effort to restrain Sherem and to hold back the disruptive potential of Sherem's influence. However, by doing so, Jacob also blocks the arrival of what would put an end to the instability Sherem has created. At the peak of their conflict with one another, Sherem asks Jacob to show him some proof or, as he says, a "sign" that Jacob's experience of the divine is something that Sherem himself could experience (Jacob 7:13). Jacob responds to Sherem's request for a sign by saying: "What am I that I should tempt God to show unto thee a sign. . . . Nevertheless not my will be done; but if God shall smite thee, let that be a sign unto thee that he hath power. . . . And thy will, O Lord, be done, and not mine" (v. 14). Jacob steps away. He erases himself. His will, his desires, his ability to influence the situation—these are all at an end. At the same time, however, he sets the terms for what comes next. He asserts that, if there is a sign, it will take the form of God smiting Sherem. This is the other side of the *katechon*: it both brings to pass a delivery from evil through its own erasure, even as it also constrains the appearance of the messiah that delivers.

As I said above, however, this story does not straightforwardly work as an eschatological allegory. Immediately following the divine arrival of redemption in the form of a sign, conditions of instability return and the *katechon* returns to its place of restraining evil. This is a depiction of a continual *katechon*, of an oscillation between restrained evil and divine presence. We see a fascinating glimpse here of the space between the removal of the *katechon* and the arrival of the messiah. Here, messianic arrival is not figured as a singular event. It is not teleological but recursive. In short, it is a form of messianic arrival that is woven into the life of a believer. There is an oscillation at work between a time of tension and restraining of evil and a time of messianic presence. Jacob 7 can thus be understood as describing what an experience of messianic presence is like: it appears, but it also recedes. The *katechon* does the work of both preventing evil and then paradoxically enabling the experience of that messianic presence. Jacob ensures that this back and forth between instability and stability, restraint and presence, or hopelessness and hope is clear by structuring the final verses accordingly and by drawing our attention to them in the introductory heading.

If we examine the verses that come after the Sherem narrative in Jacob 7, beginning with verse 23, an oscillating pattern emerges between a hopeful and hopeless outlook:

Table 1. Pattern in Jacob 7:23–27

23	peace and the love of God	hopeful
24	it all were vain	hopeless
25	trusting in the God and rock of their salvation	hopeful
26	mourn out our days	hopeless
27	hoping that many of my brethren may read my words	hopeful

This movement between hopeful and hopeless is not contradictory or manic. Rather, it illustrates how the messianic time permeates this chapter and these verses in particular. It is a manifestation of the repeated way in which the chapter shifts back and forth between stability and instability.

Messianic oscillation: Part two

An additional way of seeing this oscillating dynamic is to view it not as staging a progression but as a conception of a certain mode of theological thought. Verses 7:20–21 are marked by a kind of nonsequentiality:

> And it came to pass that when he had said these words, [Sherem] could say no more and he gave up the ghost.
>
> And when the multitude had witnessed that he spake these things as he was about to give up the ghost, they were astonished exceedingly, insomuch that the power of God came down upon them and they were overcome, that they fell to the earth. (Jacob 7:20–21)

The sequence of events here is as follows: (1) Sherem speaks to the people, confessing his wrongdoing (Jacob 7:19), (2) he stops speaking,

(3) Sherem dies, (4) the people are astonished as Sherem speaks, and (5) they fall to the earth again while Sherem is still speaking. In other words, verse 21 moves back in time. Sherem dies in verse 20 but then he is alive again in 21. This shuffling of sequence is a technique that accounts for both Sherem's experience as well as the people's experience collectively, but it is also a reordering of time. It is a mode of nonsequential temporality. Verses 20 and 21 are slippery temporally. In an important sense, they occur concurrently and not sequentially. Here, the order of events is not tied to the order of their presentation. Conceptually they occur at the same time, even if linguistically they occur in sequence.

While not as overt, this same nonsequential temporality may be at play in verses 23 and 24, where we have a moment of triumph in Jacob 7:23 followed by a return of instability in 7:24. Working along these same lines, I suggest that we read the Sherem story and Jacob's failure with the Lamanites as happening concurrently rather than sequentially. In other words, I'm suggesting that the verses could appear in either order and would still carry the same meaning. Jacob is, then, not moving from a state of triumph/stability to a state of despair/instability; rather, he is juxtaposing the two in the same moment, in the same "now." If this were a film we would have a split screen where each state would be depicted as occurring simultaneously with the other. The triumph exists in the same "now" as the despair. It seems to me that verse 24 provides no causal link from the previous events as a ground for the actions with the Lamanites. Instead, I think that the *katechonic* logic of destroying continually in verse 24 signals that a more than chronological form of time is in play.

Jacob moves back and forth from the hopeful to the precarious to highlight that in messianic time hope and despair are not oppositional but rather absorbed into a different mode of experience. This mirrors how Agamben describes kairos and chronos as collapsing into one another in messianic time.[21] Jacob oscillates both temporally (as in Jacob 7:20 and 21) as well as conceptually (between hope and despair) to demonstrate his thinking about the messiah who operates in paradox.

---

21. Agamben, *Time That Remains,* 68–69, 142.

Time is, in general, slippery and ambiguous in the book of Jacob. Jacob 7:1 reports that Sherem appeared "after some years had passed away," but he gives no reference point. Some years after what? Then, after Sherem encounters the divine in the form of a sign, we're told that he is "nourished for the space of many days" (Jacob 7:15). But how many is "many?" A week? A month? Years? Jacob provides temporal markers like "years" and "days," but we have no scale of time for these events. Similarly, the chapter summaries tell us that the book of Jacob covers, somehow, a span of 123 years. This ambiguity arises because we are given so little narrative and so few events to anchor the reader to a clear timeline. Time becomes so strange that the events from the time Jacob receives the plates to the time his son Enos has grown old and is about to die could potentially take place over a 120-year span. The katechon ruptures time. Time becomes loose and indeterminate.

In Jacob 7:26 and 27, a similar indeterminacy and paradox is also visible. These verses mirror the oscillation seen in verses 23 and 24, where the verses move between despair and hope:

> And it came to pass that I Jacob began to be old. And the record of this people being kept on the other plates of Nephi, wherefore I conclude this record, declaring that I have written according to the best of my knowledge, by saying that the time passed away with us, and also our lives passed away like as it were unto us a dream, we being a lonesome and a solemn people, wanderers cast out from Jerusalem, born in tribulation, in a wild wilderness, and hated of our brethren, which caused wars and contentions; wherefore, we did mourn out our days.
>
> And I Jacob saw that I must soon go down to my grave; wherefore I said unto my son Enos: Take these plates. And I told him the things which my brother Nephi had commanded me, and he promised obedience unto the commands. And I make an end of my writing upon these plates, which writing hath been small. And to the reader I bid farewell, hoping that many of my brethren may read my words. Brethren, adieu. (Jacob 7:26–27)

In verse 26, Jacob's comment bleakly focuses on how he and his people are lonesome, cast out, and hated, which causes them to "mourn out [their] days." Contrast that bleakness with the vitality of verse 27 where Jacob talks about family, expresses hope, and even introduces a new character, his son Enos. In this sense, verse 26 marks the figural removal of the katechon and 27 the figural arrival of the messiah. Verse 27 also then contrasts with 7:1 where Jacob introduces Sherem. In verse 1 Jacob introduces a character who wants to displace him, but in the last verse he introduces a character, Enos, who wants to sustain him. In the first we have rejection, in the last we have devotion. Verse 26 speaks of Jacob's people distantly as "this people," but verse 27 contrasts that distancing language of "this people" with the intimacy of the language of kinship, with "my son," with a brother to whom Jacob is devoted, and with brethren whom he wishes well and commends to God. "This people" in 26 becomes sons, brothers, and community in 27. There is connection, futurity, community, and hope in this messianic verse. The messiah has arrived in verse 27.

I believe we can read Jacob as setting up an argument for how every dark moment, every moment of suffering or despair, is also a moment of potential joy and peace. His messianism doesn't play out in these verses as one of final rewards but as one that punctuates the reality of suffering with hope and redemption. The messiah for him is not beyond suffering but is in the suffering.

The book of endings

The oscillating and ambiguous conclusion to Jacob 7 embodies a dynamic that is legible throughout the book of Jacob. The book of Jacob is a book of many endings. As result, it has no final and singular ending. Rather, it gestures towards the messianic possibility of an ending that has already arrived.

Jacob chapters 1–3 conclude with Jacob announcing that "I make an end" (Jacob 3:14). Then again in chapters 4–6, Jacob appears to conclude his book by saying, "I bid you farewell. . . . Amen" (Jacob 6:13). And then, finally, chapter 7 has two endings of its own—one in verse 26 where Jacob says, "I conclude this record" (Jacob 7:26) and another in verse 27 where he says, "I make an end. . . . Adieu." Why so many endings? We might read these repeated endings as having theological significance. Their repetition subverts the finality of endings and opens the possibility that endings can always be ruptured and postponed.

We might also note how Jacob's concluding words are duplicated in the words of the Book of Mormon's final narrator, Moroni, who seems to feel a profound kinship with Jacob.

> Finally, *I bid you farewell* until I shall *meet you before the pleading bar of God*, which bar striketh the wicked with awful dread and fear. *Amen.* (Jacob 6:13)

> And now *I bid unto all farewell.* I soon go to rest in the paradise of God until my spirit and body shall again reunite and I am brought forth triumphant through the air to *meet you before the pleading bar of the great Jehovah*, the Eternal Judge of both quick and dead. *Amen.* (Moroni 10:34)

Moroni, like Jacob, expresses some of those same bleak, final thoughts in his comments about being alone to tell the sad tale of his people. But it may be even more significant that Moroni's quotation of Jacob's ending concludes the entire Book of Mormon. These verses are the only two instances in the entire Book of Mormon that use the phrase "before the pleading bar." Moroni himself, in his final words, may be invoking messianic time by including in his ending an explicit reference to another ending—an ending that, in Jacob 6:13, is itself not quite an ending. Agamben tells us that "messianic time is neither the complete nor the incomplete, neither the past nor the future, but the inversion of both."[22] This may well be Jacob's own project. The *katechon* in Jacob is figured in the phrase "to destroy us continually," but it is also manifest in the endings that do not end. There is something holding back a clear ending. Jacob 7 tells us the story of Sherem. And yet, even after this story is completed, something else remains to be said.

---

22. Agamben, *Time That Remains*, 75.

Parting words

Second Nephi and Jacob are largely sermonic, yet there is a kind of narrative remnant appended to them in Jacob 7. For my part, that remainder invokes the messiah, a messiah who cannot be fully included nor completely shut out. Perhaps Jacob 7 is best read as a messianic sermon rather than a narrative. It is a narrative that is not a narrative, an ending that is not an ending, a destruction that is not a destruction.

The *katechon* is a time without sequence, a *kairos* that absorbs and transforms a *chronos*, a messianic presence that opens chronology to its present-tense fulfillment. Though it is not the second coming, the *katechon* allows the messiah to arrive in the now of our lived experience. The *katechon* is the name of the mechanism whereby messianic presence appears and recedes in the lived experience of time. Both the form and the content of Jacob 7 foreground a messianic presence that dissipates and arrives repeatedly, and in this repetition we see the katechonic mechanism interplaying with the lived experience of the messiah. The messiah will come at the end of time, but it is also true that the messiah has always been present. The messiah is present so long as people look forward to his coming as though he had already arrived; he's present when people look forward backwardly. The messiah will one day appear. The messiah is arriving. The messiah has been here all along.

Weeping for Zion

Joseph M. Spencer

READERS OF THE BOOK OF MORMON ARE FAMILIAR with the morose conclusion to the book of Jacob. Marilyn Arnold cites the passage as evidence of Jacob's "unusually tender" nature,[1] and John Tanner uses it to exhibit "the sensitivity, vulnerability, and quiet eloquence" of this minor Book of Mormon prophet.[2] Hugh Nibley called Jacob's final words a "solemn dirge,"[3] Sidney Sperry wrote of the "sincere nature" of the farewell,[4] and Terry Warner has said that Jacob's conclusion betrays the "emotional and spiritual tribulation" that "never ended for Jacob."[5] In a creative "street-legal version" of the Book of Mormon, Michael Hicks has more recently reworded Jacob's farewell in part as follows: "We always talked about rejoicing but were mostly

---

1. Marilyn Arnold, "Unlocking the Sacred Text," *Journal of Book of Mormon Studies* 8/1 (1999): 52.

2. John S. Tanner, "Literary Reflections on Jacob and His Descendants," in *The Book of Mormon: Jacob through Words of Mormon, To Learn with Joy*, ed. Monte S. Nyman and Charles D. Tate Jr. (Provo, UT: BYU Religious Studies Center, 1990), 267.

3. Hugh W. Nibley, *Teachings of the Book of Mormon: Transcripts of Lectures Presented to an Honors Book of Mormon Class at Brigham Young University 1988–1990* (Provo, UT: FARMS, 1993), 1:409.

4. Sidney B. Sperry, *The Book of Mormon Compendium* (Salt Lake City: Bookcraft, 1968), 267.

5. C. Terry Warner, "Jacob," in *The Book of Mormon: "It Begins with a Family"* (Salt Lake City: Deseret Book, 1983), 44.

overserious and glum. We had this promised land, this New Canaan, but felt sad and put down and unfulfilled all the time. I hate to end this way. But it's true. Honest. Plain."[6] Few miss the opportunity, it seems, to highlight the almost depressive nature of Jacob's closing words.

In the following pages, however, I would like to propose a rather different reading of Jacob's farewell. He mourned, and he felt time's passage like a dream, but what might we learn if we were to read these as *normative* experiences—not as the peculiar feelings of a despairing individual, but as something Jacob as a prophet models and that we should strive to emulate? Might we outline a theology of mourning that recognizes the positive and the productive in Jacob's relation to the world? In line with certain early (and other not-so-early) Christian thinkers, I want to outline here a theology of what I will call *consecrated melancholy*. Or rather, borrowing from the language of a revelation to and about Joseph Smith, I want to begin to work out the meaning of *weeping for Zion*.[7]

I will proceed as follows. In the first section, I will investigate the basic structures that underlie Jacob 7:26. My aim in doing so is to reveal some of the complexity of the passage, but also and especially to bring out the possibility that the core of Jacob's farewell exhibits a kind of progression from one psychological diagnosis of the Nephite condition to another—the first presented only in a simile but the second presented as the actual psychological state of Jacob and his people. In a

---

6. Michael Hicks, *The Street-Legal Version of Mormon's Book* (Provo, UT: Tame Olive Press, 2012), 105.

7. The passage is to be found in Doctrine and Covenants 21:7–8: "For thus saith the Lord God: Him [Joseph Smith] have I inspired to move the cause of Zion in mighty power for good, and his diligence I know, and his prayers I have heard. Yea, his weeping for Zion I have seen, and I will cause that he shall mourn for her no longer; for his days of rejoicing are come unto the remission of his sins, and the manifestations of my blessings upon his works." For some helpful context regarding what "Zion" meant to the early Saints before the revelation concerning the actual building of a New Jerusalem, see Kerry Muhlestein, "One Continuous Flow: Revelations surrounding the 'New Translation,'" in *The Doctrine and Covenants: Revelations in Context, the 37th Annual Brigham Young University Sidney B. Sperry Symposium*, ed. Andrew H. Hedges, J. Spencer Fluhman, and Alonzo L. Gaskill (Provo, UT: BYU Religious Studies Center and Deseret Book, 2008), 40–65.

second section, I will then provide a detailed philosophical assessment of the two psychological conditions mentioned by Jacob. My intention will be to clarify the basic nature of melancholy and to spell out in a preliminary way what it might mean for melancholy to be consecrated. Finally, in a third section, I will draw out what I take to be the significance of the focus of Nephite mourning, according to Jacob. The point of this last section will be to develop as fully as possible the idea of consecrated melancholy and to bring out with real force the normative features of Jacob's and his people's morose spirit.

Some questions of structure

The words Jacob uses to bid his readers farewell are deeply familiar. Unfortunately, for all its apparent familiarity, the passage's complexity passes largely unnoticed by readers. It deserves quotation in full here, since we will be looking at it in great detail:

> And it came to pass that I, Jacob, began to be old, and the record of this people being kept on the other plates of Nephi—wherefore, I conclude this record, declaring that I have written according to the best of my knowledge, by saying that the time passed away with us, and also our lives passed away, like as it were unto us a dream, we being a lonesome and a solemn people, wanderers cast out from Jerusalem, born in tribulation in a wild wilderness, and hated of our brethren—which caused wars and contentions. Wherefore, we did mourn out our days. (Jacob 7:26)[8]

At first, perhaps, the passage reads as highly disorganized, a kind of haphazard concatenation of anxieties that serially witness to Jacob's poignant feelings. Closer investigation, however, shows that it follows

---

8. Throughout this essay, I use as a base text—but with my own punctuation and capitalization—Royal Skousen, ed., *The Book of Mormon: The Earliest Text* (New Haven: Yale University Press, 2009).

a careful plan and that a remarkably tight structure organizes the cul-
minating "saying" toward which it works.

In broadest terms, a triple intention animates the passage. Three
successive verbs organize this triple intention: "to conclude," "to
declare," and "to say." Isolating the part of the passage in which these
three verbs appear in rapid succession should help to clarify this point:
"I *conclude* this record, *declaring* that I have written according to the
best of my knowledge, by *saying* that . . ." Each of these moments might
be considered in turn. Jacob unsurprisingly states at the outset of this
fragment that the point of his farewell is to accomplish *a gesture of
conclusion*: "I conclude this record." But he then immediately qualifies
this move by making *a solemn declaration* regarding the relationship
between his personal knowledge and the record he aims to conclude:
"declaring that I have written according to the best of my knowledge."
And then, apparently because he recognizes the destabilizing effect of
his declaration, he finally offers *a clarifying saying* intended to justify
any disparity between "the best of [his] knowledge" and simple reality:
"by saying that . . ." A gesture of conclusion, secured by a solemn declaration, which then requires a clarifying saying—these are the basic
elements of the plan underlying Jacob 7:26.[9]

Of the three elements of this plan, the second is the simplest.
This is because the first, the gesture of conclusion, arises with an odd
introductory *wherefore* in the middle of what seems at first to be an
interrupted thought, while the third element, the clarifying saying, has
as its content the whole remainder of the verse with its own independent
structure. Only the solemn declaration comes across as straightforward: the expression of an entirely understandable desire for readers

---

9. Jacob shares with Moroni a sense of uncertainty when it comes to concluding his
writings. Both seem to have concluded their respective contributions to the Nephite
record three distinct times: Jacob at the end of Jacob 3, Jacob 6, and Jacob 7; and Moroni
at the end of Mormon 9, Ether 15, and Moroni 10. It might be significant that both Jacob
and Moroni write in a kind of supplementary fashion, very much in the shadow of a far
more prolific and unquestionably primary author (respectively Nephi and Mormon).
For an illuminating discussion of Moroni's struggles to conclude his contribution to
the Book of Mormon, see Grant Hardy, *Understanding the Book of Mormon: A Reader's
Guide* (New York: Oxford University Press, 2010), 248–67.

to recognize Jacob's sincerity and good faith. The other two elements therefore deserve closer scrutiny. I aim here, of course, primarily to investigate the theological force of the clarifying saying (the third element), since there Jacob outlines the Nephite experience of time's passing and the psychological conditions that attend it. Nonetheless, before turning directly to the saying and its fascinating structure, I would like to say a few words about the context of the gesture of conclusion that opens the verse. At the very least, an illuminating reading of that first element of the triple plan of Jacob 7:26 should help to motivate close and charitable reading when we turn to the saying meant to clarify the solemn declaration that accomplishes the gesture of conclusion.

Jacob's gesture of conclusion seems, at best, oddly introduced. Were the opening part of the passage to be lacking the incomplete thought regarding "the record . . . kept on the other plates of Nephi," it would read far more naturally: "And it came to pass that I, Jacob, began to be old, . . . wherefore, I conclude this record." The difficulty, of course, is that Jacob inserts between his statement regarding death's approach and his gesture of conclusion a straying aside that appears never to be completed: "and the record of this people being kept on the other plates of Nephi . . ." This clause seems to be either unrelated to the rest of the verse or inexplicably but definitively abandoned before its relevance ever manifests itself. But a closer reading, one invested in questions of structure, points to apparent motivations for Jacob's inclusion of the odd clause. A triple contrast establishes a close relationship between the statement regarding the "other plates" and Jacob's gesture of conclusion. Parallel to the phrase "the other plates" in the apparently stray clause is Jacob's reference to "this record" in the gesture of conclusion. A similar parallel exists between "this people" in the apparently stray clause and the first personal "I" in the gesture of conclusion. Finally, the gerundive "being kept" of the apparently stray clause stands in parallel to the conjugated "conclude" of the gesture of conclusion. It should be noted that these parallels follow one after another in rather strict order, which suggests that they are to be read as intentional.

the record of [this people] [being kept] on [the other plates of Nephi]

[I] [conclude] [this record]

All these parallels are contrastive in nature. Jacob seems intent
on distinguishing himself, an individual prophet, from the undiffer-
entiated mass of individuals making up "this people." His gesture of
conclusion ("I conclude"), moreover, stands in contrast to the ongoing
work of keeping a national chronicle ("being kept"). And this, finally,
underscores the essential difference between "this record," Jacob and
Nephi's small plates with their overarching theological programs,[10] and
"the other plates of Nephi," the ever-proliferating annals of the Nephite
people.[11] All these details make clear the close relationship between
Jacob's gesture of conclusion and the only apparently stray clause that
immediately precedes it. Moreover, the nature of the overarching contrast between the individual prophet who concludes his programmatic
record and the nonindividualized people who keep their chronicle in
an ongoing fashion marks the relevance of the still-earlier reference
to Jacob's approaching death. Individuals grow old and face death,
but peoples do not (or do so only seldom, and then under extreme circumstances).[12] The contrastive parallels between the second and third
clauses of the verse rest on the foundation of the death announcement
of the first clause of the verse.

Structural analysis of the opening lines of Jacob 7:26 exhibits remark-
able explanatory power. What at first reads as sloppy and directionless
ultimately reveals itself as complex and even sophisticated.[13] There is

---

10. I have written extensively about the overarching theological program of Nephi
and Jacob's small plates. See Joseph M. Spencer, *An Other Testament: On Typology*
(Salem, OR: Salt Press, 2012), 33–104.

11. Statements regarding the differences between the two Nephite records can be
found in 1 Nephi 9:2–5 and 1 Nephi 19:1–5.

12. Jacob's Nephites, of course, would eventually face extinction, at a point when
they had grown "ripe," as the text says (Helaman 13:14), but that time was in the distant
future for Jacob—even if he had himself prophesied of it (see Jacob 3:3).

13. It seems to me possible to explain even the odd gerundive construction of the
second clause's "being kept" in light of these structural points. One most naturally takes

much already in the opening lines of verse 26 that can be clarified greatly by paying close attention to structure. This is all the truer when attention turns from Jacob's gesture of conclusion to the clarifying saying that makes up the largest and most detailed part of the verse—the part of the verse to which we will give focused theological attention throughout the rest of this paper. I would like to turn to this clarifying saying now.

At the broadest level, it should be said that Jacob's clarifying saying, meant to explain the possible disparity between his account and history itself, contains three simple parts: two distinct psychologically fraught statements regarding time's passing (first, "the time passed away with us, and also our lives passed away, like as it were unto us a dream," and second, "we did mourn out our days"), and one complex description of the Nephite worldview ("a lonesome and a solemn people, wanderers cast out from Jerusalem, born in tribulation in a wild wilderness, and hated of our brethren—which caused wars and contentions"). These are the basic parts of the saying. In terms of sequence, however, Jacob positions the description of the Nephite worldview between the two statements regarding time's passing, using brief rhetorical gestures to mark transitions between parts:

---

such a construction to render the first of two clauses grammatically dependent on but explanatorily foundational for the second: "X being Y, Z must be the case." The difficulty in Jacob's farewell is, first, that the gerundive clause ("the record of this people being kept on the other plates of Nephi") reads as if it were dependent on some clause that is never stated and, second, that it seems to be in no way explanatorily foundational for the independent clause that follows it ("wherefore, I conclude this record"). The series of contrastive parallels already enumerated go some distance in alleviating these difficulties, but they do not seem to go far enough since the rhetorical construction of the verse suggests a still tighter connection. But the structural points highlighted above indicate the possibility of another interpretation. Annals and chronicles have no *one* keeper and no *identifiable* set of keepers (until the whole people have become fully extinct, anyway). Might it then be better to regard "being kept" not as a gerundive construction that marks the second clause as subordinate to the third (or to some other clause that never appears in the text) but rather as an oddly but meaningfully constructed independent clause—one that deliberately removes the grammatical subject and then eliminates the verb's indicative status by granting it instead an imperfect aspect (in the grammatical sense)?

[statement] The time passed away with us, and also our lives
passed away, like as it were unto us a dream,
    [transition] we being
        [description] a lonesome and a solemn people, wanderers cast
        out from Jerusalem, born in tribulation in a wild wilderness,
        and hated of our brethren—which caused wars and contentions.
    [transition] Wherefore,
    [statement] we did mourn out our days.

This, then, provides the most basic structural organization of the saying. Much more, however, can and should be said about structure here.

First, it seems best to see Jacob's description of the Nephite worldview as dividing rather naturally into four parts: (1) "a lonesome and
a solemn people," (2) "wanderers cast out from Jerusalem," (3) "born
in tribulation in a wild wilderness," and (4) "hated of our brethren—
which caused wars and contentions." A relatively clear logic organizes
this fourfold sequence. Jacob follows (1) the basic character of the
Nephite people of his day with (2) a word regarding their prehistory
and (3) an explanation of their own beginnings, all this leading up to
(4) their devastating ongoing condition: the unending conflict between
Nephites and Lamanites. Jacob tells a kind of story here, that of a solemn people engaged in eternal warfare with their brothers in direct
consequence of their having come into a world of conflict in exile. Jacob
and his generation were born too late to see better days in Jerusalem,
just as they were born too early to pass by the difficulties of travel and
daily family conflict. The central description that lies at the heart of the
clarifying saying of Jacob 7:26, then, provides what might be called the
fourfold nature of Jacob's way of being, as well as that of his people—
those of his peculiar generation.

This first further elaboration of the structure of Jacob's clarifying saying opens immediately onto a second. The transitional markers
noted above clearly indicate a very specific relationship between this
quadruply traumatic core of Nephite being and the Nephite experience
of time's passing, described in the opening and closing statements of
the saying. The "we being" that marks the transition from the first
statement to the description of the Nephite worldview clearly serves to

indicate that the traumas listed in the latter underlie the psychologically complex experience indicated in the former. Time passed like a dream for the Nephites precisely because they were a lonesome and a solemn people, and so on. Similarly, the "wherefore" that marks the transition from the description of the Nephite worldview to the second statement regarding time's passing indicates that the same traumas underlie the psychologically troubled experience laid out at the verse's end. The Nephites mourned out their days precisely because they were a lonesome and a solemn people, and so on. Thus Jacob clearly wants his readers to understand that the traumas reported in the description at the saying's heart ultimately lie behind his people's psychologically fraught experience of time's passing—which is described in two parallel statements.

We might, in light of these comments, put a finer point or two on the overarching structure of Jacob's clarifying saying. The fourfold nature of Nephite trauma can be more fully articulated by lining up the several clauses of the description as sequential statements. Further, the transition markers might be presented as indicating the causal relationship between the traumatic condition of the Nephites of Jacob's generation and their psychologically complicated experience of time's passing, presented in two distinct statements. Further, the parallel presentation of those two statements might be productively marked. In all, then, the structure of Jacob 7:26, as visually represented here, brings out much more of the complexity of Jacob's saying.

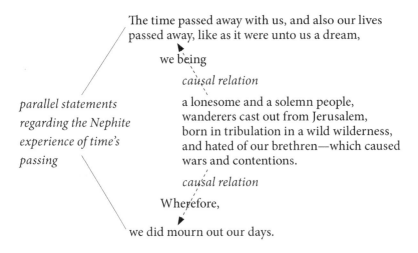

The time passed away with us, and also our lives
passed away, like as it were unto us a dream,

we being

causal relation

parallel statements
regarding the Nephite
experience of time's
passing

a lonesome and a solemn people,
wanderers cast out from Jerusalem,
born in tribulation in a wild wilderness,
and hated of our brethren—which caused
wars and contentions.

causal relation

Wherefore,

we did mourn out our days.

Now, so much structural investigation demands that an answer be given to a question too seldom asked (or too noncommittally asked) when attention focuses on structure: *What light do these structural features of Jacob's clarifying saying shed on its meaning?* Because the structure outlined above exhibits at least loosely chiastic features, we must avoid the temptation to provide this question with what has become among Latter-day Saints a too-ready answer, an answer based on a rather popular understanding of chiastic structure. One too readily claims that every chiasm privileges whatever lies at its center as somehow focal, the whole point of the use of structure. But examples abound of chiasms where the point of utilizing the textual structure seems to be otherwise: in some cases to emphasize a certain mirroring or intertwining of ideas (a good example is Isaiah 5:7: "For the vineyard of the Lord of hosts is the house of Israel, and the men of Judah his pleasant plant"); in other cases to set up boundaries within a textual unit (as in the chiastic framing of Alma 36, according to a reading I have defended elsewhere);[14] in still other cases to highlight the formal or even ritual flavor of what is said (for instance, in Nephi's oath to Zoram in 1 Nephi 4:32: "If he would hearken unto my words, as the Lord liveth, and as I live, even so that if he would hearken unto our words, we would spare his life"); and in yet still other cases to trace a transformation or inversion of things (as in the common scriptural formula, "the first shall be last and the last shall be first"). If there is in fact reason to stress the loosely chiastic structure of Jacob's clarifying saying—and this remains unsure—it has to be asked which of these purposes might underlie the structural features of the text.

Evidently, Jacob's way of structuring his clarifying saying has little to do with emphasizing or otherwise privileging what lies at its structural heart. The point of the saying in the first place is to help explain the existence of any possible discrepancy between actual history and what Jacob reports of history in his record. And this he accomplishes primarily in the opening and closing statements of the clarifying saying, not in the structurally central description of the Nephite worldview. The context privileges Jacob's attempts at identifying the

---

14. See Spencer, *An Other Testament*, 2–7.

Nephites' psychological condition, not his identification of that condition's underlying cause. For this reason, I conclude that the chief
purpose for Jacob's structuring of his clarifying saying in a loosely chiastic fashion is to trace a transformation or an inversion of sorts. I take
it that the point is to see how the dream simile of the saying's opening
statement, after a careful rehearsal of the actual traumas underlying
the Nephites' psychological condition, gives way to a more straightforward description of the Nephite experience of time's passing in terms
of mourning. Jacob's saying, it seems to me, works its way from an
approximate account of the symptoms to a more staid diagnosis of the
actual condition of the Nephites.

A glance back at the fuller visual presentation of the structure of
Jacob's saying might help to confirm this conclusion. Even as the fully
articulated structure underscores the parallel nature of the opening
and closing statements regarding the experience of time's passing,
it marks an important lack of balance between them. The opening
statement is longer and more complex. It twice attempts to state the
Nephites' experience of time's passing, in subtly but significantly different ways ("the time passed away with us," and "our lives passed away").
One cannot help but wonder whether Jacob is unsatisfied with his first
attempt at describing the experience but then also whether he ends up
just as unsatisfied with his second attempt immediately thereafter. He
goes on, of course, to compare this inadequately articulated experience
to a dream state, but he inserts between the appropriate preposition
("like") and that to which he compares the experience ("a dream")
two hesitating qualifications of the simile: "as it were" and "unto us."
With the first of these, Jacob weakens the simile, marking its artificial
character. With the second, he subjectifies the simile, limiting its force
to those undergoing the experience. All this complexity stands in stark
contrast to the unapologetic "we did mourn out our days" that closes
the verse. And the consequent imbalance of sorts between the opening
and closing statements of the clarifying saying seemingly highlights
the fact that the structure marks the transformation of a hesitant and
merely provisional attempt at clarification in the opening statement
into a confident and conclusive diagnosis in the closing statement.

With this final point regarding structure, it is perhaps possible at last to leave these merely preliminary considerations to one side and turn to philosophical or theological reflection on Jacob's clarifying saying. In the course of the saying, Jacob traces a shift from a comparison of the Nephite experience of time with having a dream to a straightforward equation of the Nephite experience of time with mourning. Perhaps the whole thing can be encapsulated in a formula of sorts: *From dreams to mourning, by way of an articulation of experienced trauma.* In the following sections, it is this summary formula, made visible thanks to close structural analysis, that will guide the following reflections above all.

On matters psychological

Interestingly, the formula of sorts with which I have concluded the above structural considerations describes not only the flow of Jacob's clarifying saying in Jacob 7:26 but also the career of the twentieth century's most influential (as well as most notorious) psychologist: Sigmund Freud. Freud's revolution in psychotherapy began in earnest when, in 1900, he announced his discovery that the analysis of dreams provided the key to discovering the unconscious.[15] The project only came to real maturity, however, beginning in 1917, when Freud finally undertook to outline what he called his metapsychology, taking his orientation at that point in his career from the experience of mourning.[16] Moreover, what drove his work on the "talking cure" was of course, from start to finish, his careful attention to what people experiencing psychological suffering had to say about their traumatic experiences. *From dreams to mourning, by way of an articulation of experienced trauma.* Jacob's attempt at diagnosing his own and his people's condition follows, peculiarly, Freud's attempt at fixing the nature of psychoanalysis.

---

15. Freud put this point this way: "The interpretation of dreams is the *via regia* [the royal road] to a knowledge of the unconscious element in our psychic life." A. A. Brill, ed. and trans., *The Basic Writings of Sigmund Freud* (New York: Modern Library, 1995), 508.

16. The key paper marking this maturation in Freud's thought is Sigmund Freud, "Mourning and Melancholia," in *Sigmund Freud, Collected Papers*, ed. Joan Riviere (New York: Basic Books, 1959), 4:152–70.

Of course, these parallels only go so far. Nonetheless, I would like to take them as a basic motivation for using Freud's thought to clarify at least some of the stakes of Jacob's references to dreams and mourning. I want to be clear, however, that I do not do so uncritically. There have been a few attempts to critique Freud from a specifically Mormon perspective, and I take these attempts seriously.[17] And psychologists in the English-speaking world have, of course, been less and less inclined to take Freud's work seriously in recent decades, something that cannot be ignored. Nonetheless, it seems to me that the development of scientific distaste for Freud, along with attempts at critique from a specifically Mormon perspective, often (and perhaps understandably) fail to recognize the richness of Freud's thought, allowing certain definitely problematic aspects of his work to get in the way of its more fruitful aspects—aspects that I think speak in particularly poignant ways to Mormon theology.[18] Perhaps if one reads Freud as a philosopher or as a thinker rather than as a scientist in the strict sense of the word, it is possible to allow his attempts at clarifying things like trauma, dreams, and mourning to inform careful reflection. It is as a philosopher that I use his work here, aware of both the danger and the promise of his thought.

To begin to assess what Jacob says about both dreams and mourning, let me first highlight again the contrast between the respective ways he refers to them. First he speaks of dreams, but only in a simile, which he further doubly qualifies. Jacob refers to dreams only to help his readers understand something that is *not* actually a dream, something

17. Most such attempts have been indirect, actually. Representative is the collection in Aaron P. Jackson, Lane Fischer, and Doris R. Dant, eds., *Turning Freud Upside Down: Gospel Perspectives on Psychotherapy's Fundamental Problems* (Provo, UT: Brigham Young University Press, 2005).

18. Although it comes with its own problems, the larger Lacanian attempt at rehabilitating Freud's work exemplifies the ability to extract the productive from the unproductive in Freud's extant writings. Perhaps more a propos, however, is the use of Freud by someone like Paul Ricoeur, who specifically investigates his relevance to philosophical reflection. See Paul Ricoeur, *Freud and Philosophy*, trans. Denis Savage (New Haven: Yale University Press, 1977). For a good introduction to the Lacanian project, see Bruce Fink, *A Clinical Introduction to Lacanian Psychoanalysis: Theory and Technique* (Cambridge, MA: Harvard University Press, 1997).

that is only dream*like*. And his qualifications of the simile ("as it were," "unto us") seem meant to underline the fact that the simile *is* just a simile. Jacob wishes his readers to understand something of the way he and his people experienced the passing of time, but he wishes just as much that his readers recognize that his illustrative images are *only* images. All this contrasts sharply with the way Jacob subsequently talks about mourning. There he leaves off similes for direct description. He and his people actually *did* mourn out their days. They *really* experienced time in terms of mourning. In this description, Jacob employs no image to help his readers grasp what he means to convey; he assumes they can understand the brute fact he reports to them.

The contrast here works because dreaming and mourning share certain features, even as they differ in important respects.[19] Their differences are, of course, much more obvious than their similarities. Dreams occur while we sleep, when our conscious awareness of the world retreats and our unconscious desires make themselves manifest. The work of mourning, on the other hand, unfolds while we remain conscious—in fact, all *too* conscious, due to the depth of our loss; in mourning we are entirely aware of our desires, the intensity of which often keeps us awake at night. And this is only the first of several obvious differences. We experience mourning in a focused way, our loss providing everything in life with a kind of focal point, deeply painful. But we experience dreams as profoundly disjointed and nonlinear, moving by metaphorical leaps and metonymical bounds.[20] Where mourning seldom gives us any reprieve from the mental effort it requires, keeping us focused on what has slipped from our grasp, dreams present us with uncanny associations and comforting discontinuities—or even abruptly conclude, allowing us to wake up when they become too horrific. Other obvious differences might be named

---

19. The similarities between dreaming and mourning explicitly motivated Freud's investigation of the latter. See Freud, "Mourning and Melancholia," 152.

20. Freud used the technical terms *displacement* and *condensation* to describe the connections and disconnections that organize the experience of dreaming. Jacques Lacan has usefully shown that these two terms map nicely onto the linguistic notions of metaphor and metonymy. See Jacques Lacan, *Écrits: The First Complete Edition in English*, trans. Bruce Fink (New York: Norton, 2006), 412–41.

too. It certainly must be said that mourning is a difficult and painful process, even if it eventually results in healing. Dreams, however, while they might at times take the shape of nightmares, are often enough pleasurable experiences or at least entirely neutral, letting us forget most of them. Further, we might note that mourning usually comes to an end, while we go on dreaming throughout our lives.

All these differences are important, but the network they form is woven also of crucial similarities. For instance, despite the obvious disjointedness of dreams, which seems to distance them absolutely from the focused experience of mourning, it must ultimately be said that a disguised coherence underpins every dream. All of a dream's metaphoric disruptions and metonymic concatenations organize them-selves into a network whose center of gravity is some kind of trauma. Whether as simple and quotidian as a passing desire for something one lacks, or whether as complex and deep as horrified fascination with self-destruction, *some* kind of trauma serves as the principle—both causal and organizational—of every dream.[21] And it is this center of gravity in every experience of dreaming that links dreams to mourning. As dreams organize a whole network of (imagistic) associations around some kind of trauma, ostensibly in an attempt to help us cope with our frustrated or forbidden or frightening desires, the work of mourning undertakes to revise the network of our conscious associations around the experience of deep loss. Confronted with the frustration of intense desires to be with a loved one, working through the forbidden anger we feel toward the one who has abandoned us, and coming to recognize the frightening fragility of life as we know it, we mourn.[22] In essence,

---

21. It is an open question whether the initially indiscernible coherence of a dream is a feature of the dream as originally and unconsciously experienced, or whether it is instead only a feature of the dream as reconstructed afterward and in a conscious state. This is, of course, an important distinction for the psychoanalyst, but it seems to me unnecessary to give it detailed attention here.

22. Freud's succinct description of the work of mourning is perhaps worth citing: "Each single one of the memories and hopes which bound the libido to the object is brought up and hyper-cathected, and the detachment of the libido from it accom-plished. . . . When the work of mourning is completed the ego becomes free and unin-hibited again." Freud, "Mourning and Melancholia," 154. Another helpful description

the work of dreaming is like the work of mourning because, in each case, we find ourselves maneuvering a landscape organized around what seems impossible to speak about—or, at least, what seems impossible to speak about without somehow committing an act of sacrilege. In dreaming as in mourning, we work out our relationship to what remains inaccessible to us.

Despite important differences in outward appearance, then, dreams and mourning share much that is essential. Jacob can make sense for his readers of his people's response to their traumatic circumstances in terms either of dreams or of mourning—although, as we have seen, it is quite clear that he means to claim that his people actually mourned, while their experience was only like dreaming. That Jacob provides his readers with *both* the simile and the direct description, asking them to understand his people's experience in terms of *both* dreaming and mourning, is important because it draws attention to the shared underlying structure of the two sorts of experience. Were Jacob only to speak of mourning, readers might too easily take him to mean just that his people grumbled about their less-than-perfect circumstances. But because he couples mourning with dreams, it becomes clear that his talk of mourning indeed bears psychological significance. His and his people's time was occupied by actual mourning, by the slow process of transformation that aims at eventually stabilizing one's affairs despite deep loss. For this reason, their experience was not *actually* that of dreaming, though it was apparently very much *like* dreaming.

Implicit in the preceding few paragraphs is what seems to be the major motivation for Jacob's nonetheless drawing a contrast between dreaming and mourning in attempting to describe his generation's experience. The very first point of difference we drew above between the two sorts of experience concerns the fact that dreaming is unconscious while mourning is conscious. This distinction, presumably, plays

---

appears later in the same essay: "Reality passes its verdict—that the object no longer exists—upon each single one of the memories and hopes through which the libido was attached to the lost object, and the ego, confronted as it were with the decision whether it will share this fate, is persuaded by the sum of its narcissistic satisfactions in being alive to sever its attachment to the non-existent object." Freud, "Mourning and Melancholia," 166.

a particularly important role in the shift from mere simile to direct description in the clarifying saying of Jacob 7:26. Dreaming is, so to speak, automatic, something that happens on its own despite our conscious intentions. We might wish for dreamless sleep, but we have no guarantee that our wish will be granted. And after being rudely awakened, we might wish to return to a pleasant dream, but we are as likely as not to move on to other dreams when we return to sleep. Mourning is a different affair entirely, however. Although we seldom have control over the events that cause or motivate our mourning, the work of mourning unfolds in anything but an automatic or unconscious way. Not only are we all too aware of our desires and our consequent pain, but we work our way toward regained normalcy only by working consciously and intentionally on seeing the world in a new way. To say that the Nephite experience during Jacob's generation was only like dreaming but was actually a matter of mourning is, it would seem, to indicate that they had to focus conscious effort on grappling with what they experienced as deep loss.

Even as we make this major point of contrast explicit, however, we should note yet another feature of Jacob's clarifying saying that brings his talk of dreams and his talk of mourning into close continuity—another feature of the saying, that is, that seems to indicate why Jacob should wish to claim that his people's mourning was *like* dreaming and therefore was *unlike* mourning to some extent. The final point of difference we drew above between the two sorts of experience concerns the fact that mourning is a work that, generally speaking, comes to a kind of resolution. Mourning comes to an end when, although we remain fully aware of our loss, we have found a way of being oriented by it or to it that allows us to go on. Something like normalcy returns. Dreams, however, as products of the incorrigibly inconsistent unconscious, do not so much end as they are interrupted, always in the middle of things. We come back from our dreams to the normal world, but we do so only by leaving the world of our dreams behind. And the world of our dreams *never* achieves normalcy. Our unconscious states never work all the way through our traumas.

This marks a further point of contrast between dreams and mourning. And yet it must be said that Jacob describes his people's mourning in the closing statement of his clarifying saying in language suggestive of dreams. When he says that he and his people "did mourn out [their] days," he clearly indicates that his people's mourning never came to an end.[23] And this is quite strange. Although it is certainly possible for someone never to work all the way through the stages of mourning, and so never to achieve normalcy again, such cases are exceptional; they are, precisely, cases that are out of the ordinary. The sort of deep loss that leads to mourning certainly traumatizes, but it does not usually traumatize so deeply that it cannot be overcome. Typically speaking, one *does not* mourn out one's days. One mourns for a time, works at reconfiguring one's world for a time, and then lives on.[24] Jacob, however, clearly seems to say that his people *never ceased to mourn.* They worked, quite consciously it seems, at giving a new shape to their world, a new shape that would allow them to return to normalcy and routine.

---

23. Time's passing shows up in Jacob's talk both of dreams and of mourning, but its formulation differs. Note that in the dream simile, Jacob struggles to articulate what he has in mind. He speaks first of "the time" that passed away, but then, before he introduces the dream simile itself, he uses a different locution: "and also our lives passed away." The difference between "the time," abstract and in the singular, and "our lives," concrete and in the plural, is suggestive. Jacob seems at first unsure whether what passes should be regarded as something formal but accessible to all, or as something real but privately experienced. Whatever their differences, however, these two locutions share an important feature: objectivity. Both are sorts of things that can pass away. Jacob's formulation of time's passing in the statement that concludes his clarifying saying, however, operates in a nonobjective way. In his direct description of the experience of mourning, Jacob seems to combine the dream simile's two terms ("the time" and "our days") in a single term: "our days." This term seems to indicate something that is shared like time in general and therefore is irreducible to the privacy of a singular life, and yet that is unquestionably concrete and therefore irreducible to merely formal accessibility. Moreover, this conception of temporal experience makes time immanent to the work of mourning. It no longer passes one by, but rather is what one passes through in mourning. People "mourn out" their days. Despite these clear differences between the ways of talking about time in the opening and closing statements of Jacob's clarifying saying, however, it seems perfectly clear that the processes described in each never come to an end. Nephite mourning is dreamlike at least in the odd fact that it does not come to an end.

24. Freud notes that occasionally the "struggle" of mourning "can be so intense that a turning away from reality ensues." Freud, "Mourning and Melancholia," 154.

They worked, that is, at the possibility of being at last at their ease. But, apparently, they failed. They failed ever to live on, to breathe easily, to be consoled, to experience equilibrium. It would seem that their loss was too deep to allow them—or at least those of Jacob's generation— ever to rest.

At this point, then, it becomes necessary to ask exactly what it was that Jacob and his people lost. What was it that caused perpetual, unceasing mourning, preventing their coming to a point of rest or of normalcy? Actually, Jacob states the answer to this question quite straightforwardly in the course of his fourfold description of the traumatic experience that underlay his and his people's dreamlike mourning. What Jacob and his people lost was Jerusalem. In fact, he informs us that he and his people had a particularly odd relationship to that loss, indicated by the essential incompatibility between two things Jacob says about his people's relationship to Jerusalem. In the course of his fourfold description of Nephite trauma, he says both that they were "born . . . in a wild wilderness" and that they were "cast out from Jerusalem." The combination of these two claims, of course, makes no sense. If one has been cast out of the city of her nativity, then she must have been born there—not in "a wild wilderness." Or if she has been born elsewhere and in fact has never been to the city in question, it makes little sense to say that she has been "cast out" from it. Yet Jacob combines these two incommensurable experiences into one traumatic whole that underlies the Nephite psychological condition. His generation was at once born at a distance from Jerusalem, and yet they were always poignantly aware of their being in a kind of exile. It was thus that they "did mourn out [their] days."

I will come back to the significance of Jerusalem as the focus of Nephite loss in the final section of this paper. For the moment, it is enough just to recognize from Jacob's paradoxical description of the Nephite experience that they underwent a rather unique sort of mourning. Their mourning was not of the sort that comes to an end. Jacob and his people mourned a constitutive, irreparable loss. Helpfully, Freud has a name for this condition, or for something quite like it—a venerable name drawn, in fact, from Christian theology: *melancholia*.[25] Actually, the condition Jacob describes differs in at least one important respect from what Freud calls melancholia, since the latter emphasizes the unconscious nature of the condition as framed by psychoanalytic practice, while Jacob, with his talk of mourning, emphasizes the conscious nature of his people's experience. Perhaps precisely for this reason, it might be useful to examine melancholia from the perspective of one of Freud's more insightful critics: Giorgio Agamben. At its real heart, Agamben explains, "Melancholy would be not so much the regressive reaction to the loss of the love object [described by Freud] as the imaginative capacity to make an unobtainable object appear as if lost." The melancholic in effect "stages a simulation where what cannot be lost because it has never been possessed [nevertheless] *appears* as lost."[26] Put in other words, there lies at the heart of the melancholic experience a paradoxical transformation of the merely inaccessible into the actually lost. And this seems to me a remarkably apt characterization of the situation Jacob describes. Although he and his people had never actually seen Jerusalem, they related to it as if it had nonetheless once been theirs; they experienced it as constitutively, irreparably lost.

Not only does Agamben's slight-but-significant corrective to Freud's conception of melancholia point in the direction of Jacob 7:26, it also aims to sum up a longstanding Christian theological tradition. Agamben is explicit about the fact that the Christian tradition oddly and perhaps ironically lies behind Freud's attempt to think about melancholia. Even more usefully though, Agamben—unlike Freud—draws from that tradition to distinguish between two sorts of melancholy. There is on the one hand what early Christian thinkers called *tristitia*

---

25. See, again, Freud, "Mourning and Melancholia." It may be significant that Jacob speaks of mourning rather than, strictly speaking, of melancholia. Freud emphasizes the strictly *unconscious* nature of melancholic suffering, but Jacob's emphasis on mourning suggests the *conscious* nature of his and his people's experience.

26. Giorgio Agamben, *Stanzas: Word and Phantasm in Western Culture*, trans. Ronald L. Martinez (Minneapolis: University of Minnesota Press, 1993), 20, emphasis added.

mortifera, deadly sadness, a kind of sickness unto death.[27] And there is on the other hand what early Christian thinkers called *tristitia saluti-fera*, saving sadness, akin in certain ways to what Latter-day Saints often call godly sorrow.[28] Focusing on the latter of these two sorts of melancholy, Agamben speaks of an "obscure wisdom according to which hope has been given only for the hopeless"[29]—a formula very much resonant with my own recent attempt to lay out a Mormon theology of hope. Like Sarah and Abraham, confronted with the genuinely objective impossibility of a child, but precisely *therefore* free to hope for a child from the God who covenants to undermine the objective order of the world, it is "they that mourn" whom Jesus calls "blessed," because "they shall be comforted" (Matthew 5:4).[30] Agamben rightly says of melancholic or ceaseless mourning, "The greatest disgrace is never to have had it."[31] Or perhaps it would be most relevant to cite in this connection a formula Jacob first heard falling from the lips of his dying father, given in the form of a final blessing on the melancholic child: "In thy childhood thou hast suffered afflictions and much sorrow, . . . [but] thou knowest the greatness of God, and he shall consecrate thine afflictions for thy gain" (2 Nephi 2:1–2). From quite early in his life, Jacob knew of the possibility of a kind of *consecrated melancholy*.

How is one to distinguish between the two sorts of melancholy identified by the Christian tradition—between a sort of interminable mourning that results in the death of the soul and a sort of interminable mourning that somehow deserves commendation? What makes Joseph Smith's "weeping for Zion" a good thing (D&C 21:8) and what

---

27. I borrow this last phrase from John 11:4, but also from Søren Kierkegaard's book-length commentary on that passage. See Søren Kierkegaard, *"Fear and Trembling" and "The Sickness unto Death,"* trans. Walter Lowrie (Princeton: Princeton University Press, 1954), 133–278.

28. This language comes, of course, from 2 Corinthians 7:10.

29. Agamben, *Stanzas*, 7.

30. I draw the story of Sarah and Abraham from Paul's discussion in Romans 4. See my discussion of Paul's analysis in Joseph M. Spencer, *For Zion: A Mormon Theology of Hope* (Salt Lake City: Greg Kofford Books, 2014), 15–23.

31. Agamben, *Stanzas*, 7. Also recommended is the treatment of melancholia in Jean-Luc Marion, *God without Being*, trans. Thomas A. Carlson (Chicago: University of Chicago Press, 1991), 132–38.

Mormon calls "the sorrowing of the damned" a clearly bad thing (Mormon 2:13)? What differentiates the wandering "pilgrims" of Hebrews 11:13 from those condemned for having "loved to wander" in Jeremiah 14:10? Why should we not limit ourselves to speaking of the joy of the saints and the misery of the rebellious, avoiding the complexity implied by the fact that even the redeemed experience "sorrow . . . for the sins of the world" (3 Nephi 28:9)—not to mention the even starker complexity implied by Enoch's vision of "the God of heaven" who "looked upon the residue of the people, and . . . wept" (Moses 7:28)? How do we know whether our hearts are broken because we see that we cannot reach on our own what we nonetheless rightly desire, and when are our hearts broken because we see the impossibility of having what we should not but cannot help but desire?

There are, I suspect, dozens of good and productive answers to these questions. Leaving their enumeration for another occasion, however, I wish to focus in on just one possible answer—the one implied by Jacob's exclusive focus on what he and his people experienced as definitively lost: Jerusalem. It is well and good to speak of consecrated dreamlike mourning, but what lies behind that consecrated dreamlike mourning for Jacob is something quite specific. For the remainder of this theological investigation, I mean to ask what we might learn by turning our attention to what Jacob saw as forever lost.

Next year in Zion

Everything we have said to this point makes clear that there are at least some reasons to think that Jacob's sort of melancholy, famously on display in Jacob 7:26, is redemptive rather than lamentable. It is possible and even right to speak of consecrated melancholy, a sort of saving sadness or a mourning that aligns with God's purposes. In Jacob's own words, such mourning assumes the right shape when it takes as its object or focus Jerusalem's loss, the fact that Zion has not as yet been redeemed or rebuilt. And so, it seems, to go any further in understanding what it might mean to take Jacob's mournful spirit as a guiding spirit, it will be necessary to investigate the basic meaning of his and his people's relationship to the city of Jerusalem, to the city they had never seen but nonetheless experienced as definitively lost. To do so—that is, to seek evidence concerning Jacob's and his people's understandings of Jerusalem—we can have recourse only to Jacob's words, since he is the only person from his unique generation whose words appear in the Book of Mormon. It will be necessary, then, to proceed with a survey of what Jacob has to say about the city whose inaccessibility he mourned all his life.

References to Jerusalem in the book of Jacob are few. It is perhaps telling, nonetheless, that Jacob opens his record by situating its beginnings at the time when "fifty and five years had passed away from the time that Lehi left Jerusalem" (Jacob 1:1).[32] Even before Nephi's death, but also and just as surely during the years following, it seems that the Nephites measured time itself in terms of Jerusalem's loss. That is certainly significant, but it should be noted that Jacob's formula does not, strictly speaking, refer to Jerusalem's loss. Rather, it speaks of the time that Lehi *left* Jerusalem, the family abandoning the city rather than the city exiling the family. Despite the nostalgic tone of Jacob 7:26, Jacob 1:1 suggests something of Nephite disgust for the city left behind. And what follows throughout the book of Jacob confirms this sense of antipathy for the city whose loss Jacob's final words lament so touchingly. In Jacob 4, for instance, Jacob speaks with a kind of contempt for the people of the city his family had left behind before his birth: "Behold, the Jews were a stiffnecked people, and they despised the words of plainness, and killed the prophets, and sought for things that they could not understand" (Jacob 4:14). Jacob's distaste, perhaps personal, for Jerusalem and its people is fully on display here.

Even more striking is the complex treatment of Jerusalem to be found in Jacob 2–3. There Jacob lays out less apparently personal (and therefore much more compelling) reasons for his family's having been directed to leave Jerusalem. In the course of a sermon dedicated to berating the Nephites for nascent wickedness among them—wickedness

---

32. Note that a similar formula appears in Nephi's writings in 2 Nephi 5:28. The major difference between the two is, of course, that Jacob speaks of his father's departure, while Nephi speaks of leaving Jerusalem in the plural first person.

displayed most egregiously in problematic conceptions of gender relations[33]—Jacob quotes the Lord as saying the following:

> I have led this people forth out of the land of Jerusalem
> by the power of mine arm that I might raise up unto me a
> righteous branch from the fruit of the loins of Joseph. . . .
> I the Lord have seen the sorrow and heard the mourning
> of the daughters of my people in the land of Jerusalem—
> yea, and in all the lands of my people—because of the
> wickedness and abominations of their husbands. And
> I will not suffer, saith the Lord of Hosts, that the cries
> of the fair daughters of this people, which I have led out
> of the land of Jerusalem, shall come up unto me. (Jacob
> 2:25, 31–32)

Here again the almost nostalgic feel of Jacob 7:26 is missing. Jerusalem
is less something lost that should therefore be mourned than the very
seat of wickedness, something that must be left behind to pursue true
righteousness. In the place of Nephites mourning for a lost city, one
finds in this text "the mourning of the daughters . . . of Jerusalem," the
unceasing sorrow of women who have lost confidence in "their hus-
bands." When Jacob confronts his people and their own wickedness,
he sees Jerusalem primarily as the city of "David and Solomon," whose
examples he does not hesitate to call "abominable" (Jacob 2:24).

   In none of these texts from earlier in the book of Jacob does one
find talk of the Lehites being "cast out" from Jerusalem, as in Jacob 7.
Instead, in these earlier texts, the Lehites are "led out" of the abominable city—or, as in the time-measurement of the book's opening
verse, they simply "left" the city as they sought their own promised
land. A holistic view of the book of Jacob thus seems to complicate
the deep sense of loss expressed at the book's conclusion. From the
references reviewed here, it seems unlikely that what is *really* at issue

---

33. For an analysis of these and related texts, see Joseph M. Spencer and Kimberly
M. Berkey, "'Great Cause to Mourn': The Complexity of Gender and Race in the Book
of Mormon," in *The Book of Mormon: Americanist Approaches*, ed. Jared Hickman and
Elizabeth Fenton (New York: Oxford University Press, forthcoming).

in Jacob's mournful final words in Jacob 7:26 is just the fact that the Lehite peoples are no longer acquainted with Jerusalem. There is, it seems, something more complex at work in Jacob's lament concerning his people's being "wanderers cast out from Jerusalem." The key to making better sense of this situation lies, I think, in a lengthy, well-known sermon delivered by Jacob but not included in his own book; it appears, rather, in 2 Nephi 6–10, gathered into the complex project of Nephi's written record.[34] To get to the heart of what interests Jacob when it comes to Jerusalem and its fate, it is necessary to turn from the book of Jacob to this sermon, even if its meaning has been channeled by Nephi's editorial interests.

The first reference to Jerusalem in the sermon of 2 Nephi 6–10 comes at the outset of a kind of commentary on a passage from Isaiah (specifically, Isaiah 49:22–23), a passage assigned to Jacob by Nephi as the text for his preaching. Describing the first of a series of events in Judah's history that Jacob understands to be relevant to the interpretation of the Isaiah text, he says: "The Lord hath shewn me that they which were at Jerusalem, from whence we came, have been slain and carried away captive" (2 Nephi 6:8). Two points seem especially salient here. First, Jacob cites as his source for this information regarding Jerusalem and its inhabitants a vision. Second, Jacob claims that the vision in question has given him to witness Jerusalem's fall, but this destruction of the city constitutes a loss deeper than any we have mentioned to this point, resulting in an exile of world-historical significance. Observant Jews to this day mourn *this* loss and experience *this* exile, symbolized most poignantly in the glass crushed at Jewish wedding ceremonies in memory of the destruction of Solomon's temple. As the psalmist sings of Jerusalem's destruction at Babylon's hands: "If I do not remember thee, let my tongue cleave to the roof of my mouth; if I prefer not Jerusalem above my chief joy" (Psalm 137:6).

Yet Jacob's visionary witness of Jerusalem's fall only sets up his interpretation of Isaiah, and he focuses that interpretation on

---

34. I have analyzed the structure of Nephi's record, including the role played there by Jacob's sermon, in Spencer, *An Other Testament*, 34–58. I might note that I would revise many aspects of that analysis today.

subsequent events in Jewish history. Significantly, the next three of Jacob's references to Jerusalem come in a lengthy quotation (of Isaiah 50:1–52:2), which he uses to provide context for the briefer Isaiah passage (Isaiah 49:22–23) on which he means to comment in his sermon. The first of these Isaianic references to Jerusalem echoes Jacob's own talk of destruction and exile, even as it begins to point beyond it: "Awake! Awake!" Isaiah says to Judah, "Stand up, O Jerusalem, which hast drunk at the hand of the Lord the cup of his fury!" (2 Nephi 8:17, quoting Isaiah 51:17). The other two references to Jerusalem come as a pair a few verses later in a reprise of these heartening words: "Awake! Awake! Put on thy strength, O Zion! Put on thy beautiful garments, O Jerusalem, the holy city! For henceforth there shall no more come into thee the uncircumcised and the unclean! Shake thyself from the dust! Arise, sit down, O Jerusalem! Loose thyself from the bands of thy neck, O captive daughter of Zion!" (2 Nephi 8:24–25). Beyond loss and exile, Jacob sees the promise of Jerusalem's redemption. But of course, he sees such redemption only at a distance, envisioned as occurring at a time thousands of years in the future. And so there is much to mourn in the meanwhile.

Perhaps, then, this begins to explain Jacob's mourning. And yet there is more Jacob has to say in his sermon regarding Jerusalem. After concluding his long quotation from Isaiah and immediately before pursuing a long theological tangent regarding the nature of resurrection, Jacob refers to another event associated with Jerusalem that might give him reason to mourn. "In the body [God] shall shew himself unto they at Jerusalem, from whence we came," he explains (2 Nephi 9:5). The bad news he does not give in full until further along, however. It comes with these words: "Because of priestcrafts and iniquities, they at Jerusalem will stiffen their necks against him, that he be crucified. Wherefore, because of their iniquities, destructions, famines, pestilences, and bloodsheds shall come upon them. And they which shall not be destroyed shall be scattered among all nations" (2 Nephi 10:5–6). Unfortunately (and not without a style of language that makes twenty-first-century readers uncomfortable), Jacob sees in the crucifixion of

Jesus Christ a major feature of Jerusalem's sacred history.[35] In *that* he finds reason to mourn as well. The alienation of Israel from their would-be deliverer causes him—as he explains later in his own book—a great deal of anxiety, what he even calls "overanxiety" (Jacob 4:18). It may be of real significance that such language is psychologically freighted like the language of Jacob 7:26.

Now, what is to be gathered from all these Jacobite references to Jerusalem's sad history? At the very least, it is necessary to countenance the possibility that what worried Jacob and his people was *less their own* distance from Jerusalem than the way their distance from Jerusalem symbolized the city's loss in a much larger historical sense. The exile of sorts experienced by Jacob's people was a constant reminder of the exile they had barely missed by leaving Jerusalem during Zedekiah's reign—the exile that God nonetheless showed them in vision. At the very time Lehi and his family left Jerusalem for the New World, those whom they left behind subsequently left Jerusalem for lowly exile in Babylon. And of course that exile was itself a symbol of a much larger history in which Judah has been consistently homeless and traumatized, waiting for messianic redemption.[36] This the Nephite prophets of the first generation saw clearly in their visionary experiences, and they thereby knew all too keenly that redemption for Jerusalem and the covenant people lay only in an inaccessible future, too far off to find any real joy in it.[37] The best among Jacob's people apparently mourned out

---

35. Second Nephi 10:3–6 has often been labeled anti-Semitic in tone, especially because of the claim there that "the Jews" constitute "the more wicked part of the world," a claim supposedly justified because "there is none other nation on earth that would crucify their God." Perhaps one could exonerate the Book of Mormon by noting that it goes on in the same passage to provide a further point of justification by using the language of the New Testament (such that its anti-Semitic spirit is borrowed rather than original) or by insisting that the passage explicitly limits the "wicked" to those involved in "priestcrafts and iniquities" (presumably referring just to certain opportunistic leaders). But the point stands that Jacob's language is troubling, and this should not be overlooked.

36. N. T. Wright has recently spelled out at length and quite beautifully the way the brief exile in Babylon took on larger historical meaning. See N. T. Wright, *Paul and the Faithfulness of God* (Minneapolis: Fortress Press, 2013), 1:139–63.

37. On this point, see Spencer, *For Zion*, 71–78.

their days because they were attuned to the Abrahamic in the Christian gospel, because they saw that even the Messiah's arrival could only *start* the process of redeeming Israel, as well as the process of Israel's associated redemption of the world.[38] Fulfillment would be waiting a very long time.

There is a key theological term central to the story of Jacob's encounter with Sherem that is relevant to all this talk of the covenant and its delayed fulfillment, although the term hardly appears relevant at first sight. As the encounter with Sherem unfolds, Jacob eventually testifies that his knowledge was rooted in "the power of the Holy Ghost" (Jacob 7:12), and Sherem responds by asking for a sign executed by that same power (see Jacob 7:13). Close reading of the small plates suggests that these references to "the power of the Holy Ghost" have a quite specific meaning. The phrase appears in Nephi's writings in very strategic places and with highly specific associations. Although Latter-day Saints are accustomed to conflating the power of the Holy Ghost with the witness of the Spirit of God, Nephi—and presumably therefore Jacob as well—seems to have something narrower in mind when using these words, and that something has everything to do with Jerusalem and the Abrahamic covenant.

According to Nephi, the power of the Holy Ghost is specifically that by which one can "see and hear and know" of Israel's history. He effectively promises his readers that *everyone* can have an apocalyptic vision of the world's Abrahamic history so long as they "diligently seek" it. As he says, "the mysteries of God shall be unfolded to them by the power of the Holy Ghost"—to deny this, according to Nephi, is to deny the Lord's "one eternal round" (1 Nephi 10:19), to deny that he is "the same yesterday and today and forever" (v. 18), working at one and the same massive historical project. The power of the Holy Ghost is thus not only the power by which Nephi himself witnesses in vision the whole of Israel's future; it is also a power relevant to the era in which the Book of Mormon would eventually circulate—that is, of

---

38. Third Nephi 15:1–9 serves as a kind of commentary on the mismatch between the Messiah's arrival and the longer history of Israel's redemption. It is, in many ways, the interpretive key to the remainder of the Book of Mormon.

course, our own era. In a vision of the "last days," Nephi says that "they which shall seek to bring forth [the Lord's] Zion at that day . . . shall have the gift and the power of the Holy Ghost" (1 Nephi 13:37). To be contrasted with such repentant people, according to Nephi, are those Christians who symptomatically fail to recognize that their "bible" came "from the Jews, [the Lord's] ancient covenant people" (2 Nephi 29:4). In exasperation, Nephi quotes the Lord:

> And what thank they the Jews for the bible which they receive from them? Yea, what do the gentiles mean? Do they remember the travails and the labors and the pains of the Jews—and their diligence unto me—in bringing forth salvation unto the gentiles? O ye gentiles, have ye remembered the Jews, mine ancient covenant people? Nay, but ye have cursed them and have hated them and have not sought to recover them. But behold, I will return all these things upon your own heads, for I the Lord hath not forgotten my people! (2 Nephi 29:4–5)

While culturally Christian Europe has hated and persecuted—*and massacred*—Jews, the power of the Holy Ghost, according to Nephi, has attempted to find its way into open hearts, seeking to restore a sense of the promises linked to a city now lost for thousands of years.

In closely related passages, Nephi excoriates the latter-day world, so deeply secular that even its Christians deny the power of the Holy Ghost. The symptom of this denial, Nephi says, is that they are "at ease in Zion," crying, "All is well!" (2 Nephi 28:24–25). Failing to weep for Zion, failing to mourn out their days, they—like us—ignore the very power by which one should be reminded of the Abrahamic under-pinnings of the Christian gospel. Today, it would seem, the world is made up mostly of Sherems, skeptical of revelation or of any real power of the Holy Ghost. We satisfy ourselves that all is well in Zion—or, alternatively, that there is *much* to mourn in Zion while ignoring all things Abrahamic in favor of our own moral concerns, traditional or fashionable as the case may be. We continue to forget what God claims he cannot forget. And we thereby deny the very power that Jacob says lies behind his deepest theological and existential concerns. It would seem that it was always and only by that same power—the power of the Holy Ghost—that Jacob and his people mourned in a consecrated way.

To weep for Zion, or to mourn out our days as we think of Jerusalem's loss—*this* is what, according to Jacob and Nephi, the power of the Holy Ghost would lead us to do. If they are right, then perhaps the woes they pronounced upon the last days are ones we should take most seriously. How many tears do we shed for the Zion envisaged in the Abrahamic covenant? Far too few. But perhaps, reading the small plates carefully, we might be led to shed a few more.

Covenant Obligation to Scripture as Covenant Obligation to Family

Sharon J. Harris

THIS ESSAY EXPLORES HOW JACOB 7 PORTRAYS READERS' covenant obligation to scripture and how this leads to reauthoring that obligation to the Abrahamic covenant and to family.[1] The interaction of scripture and family within a covenant framework challenges us to rethink our definition of and understanding of *family* and provides a relational theological view of family.[2]

Access to scripture

In their confrontation, perhaps at the temple, Jacob asks Sherem if he believes the scriptures, and Sherem responds that he does. But what kind of access to scripture would Sherem have had? Sherem is "learned, that he had a perfect knowledge of the language of the people," so presumably he would have had at least as much and probably more

---

1. My thanks to all the members of the 2015 seminar for their feedback and development of these ideas and for creating an environment where ideas could flourish. I am also grateful to Edward Jeter for his input on this essay.

2. See Samuel M. Brown, *First Principles and Ordinances of the Gospel: The Fourth Article of Faith in Light of the Temple* (Provo, UT: Neal A. Maxwell Institute Press, 2015); and Adam S. Miller, *Letters to a Young Mormon* (Provo, UT: Neal A. Maxwell Institute, 2014), particularly the essay, "Sin."

interest in and access to writings and records than the common member of that society (Jacob 7:4). In the small plates, however, it seems that general access to scripture is not so common. The importance placed on obtaining the brass plates, without which the people would "dwindle and perish in unbelief," suggests that the brass plates were the primary—perhaps the only—scriptural record Lehi and his family carried with them to the promised land (1 Nephi 4:13). Moreover, in the early years of Lehi's family settling the promised land, we do not have the examples of more widespread use of the scriptures that we do later in the Book of Mormon. Nephi reads the scriptures to his brethren, but he does not generally encourage them to study the scriptures themselves.[3] Contextually, even Nephi's injunction to "feast upon the words of Christ" in his closing message (2 Nephi 32:3) emphasizes the gift of the Holy Ghost and asking for understanding as the method for such feasting rather than the activity of searching the scriptures.[4] Comparatively, popular access to the sacred written record during most of Nephi's and Jacob's lifetimes seems to have been limited.

The contrast between priestly and popular access to scripture in the small plates comes into greater relief when we consider later examples from the large plates. Later in Lehite history, multiple groups had clearly taken to studying scripture. King Benjamin had his message at the temple written and distributed among all his people. In Ammonihah several scriptures were burned to punish believers. The priests of King Noah questioned Abinadi about directly quoted passages of scripture, and Abinadi responded by quoting scripture in return

---

3. When Nephi finds his brothers disputing over what Lehi has taught them in 1 Nephi 15, Nephi does not encourage them to read Isaiah in his response but recites it to them. In 1 Nephi 19, Nephi explains at some length his commandment to keep two sets of plates, his concern over potential mistakes he may make, and then quotes several prophecies and prophets from the scriptures. Clearly Nephi has access to the record, but when it comes to teaching his brethren in verses 22–23, he reads to them from the brass plates, the five books of Moses, and Isaiah. It could be that they do not have access to the scriptures except through the keeper of the plates, Nephi.

4. Perhaps the scriptures were not readily and personally available to Nephi's people during his life, and so he did not emphasize that activity and possibility to future generations as much either.

(see Mosiah 12–16). The politically elite sons of Mosiah "searched the scriptures diligently" (Alma 17:2), but this time access to scripture apparently was not limited only to those of means or with high government or ecclesiastical connections. Alma taught poor Zoramites, "Ye ought to search the scriptures," and asked them, "Have [ye] read the scriptures?" (Alma 33:2, 14). By the time of Christ's birth, there were even contentions in the church over interpretations of scripture regarding observance of the law of Moses (see 3 Nephi 1:24). All this is to say that between the time of Nephi and the time of the books of Mosiah and Alma, the people's attention to and engagement with scripture had increased.

What accounts for this shift in religious practice? The influence of Jacob, as portrayed in the account of Jacob and Sherem's confrontation in Jacob 7, provides at least a partial explanation for the shift toward greater popular engagement with scripture. Nephi says that he did "liken all scriptures unto us, that it might be for our profit and learning" (1 Nephi 19:23). In Jacob 7 we see how Jacob likened scriptures to himself through his understanding of covenants as they relate to scripture and as they are found in scripture. Thus the drama of Sherem's story demonstrates the urgency of understanding scripture and that scripture always imposes on us a covenant obligation to attend to it.

Jacob's relationship to scripture

To understand how Jacob's telling of the story of Sherem reveals the covenant nature of scripture, we first have to understand how Jacob, as narrator and author, regards scripture. Jacob feels his personal responsibility to the scriptures keenly. He opens his record by reciting the command to care for the plates from his brother Nephi, and Jacob refers to his charge over the plates as a "commandment" three times in the opening verses (Jacob 1:1, 2, 8). He also emphasizes it at the end of his narrative when he transfers the plates to his son Enos. As Jacob closes his account, he then says, "And I Jacob saw that I must soon go down to my grave, wherefore I said unto my son Enos: Take

these plates" (Jacob 7:27).[5] Jacob's direct quotation of himself is striking here; we have not heard Jacob's spoken words as a direct quotation
since Sherem was smitten several verses earlier. This seemingly random
quotation of three short words also stands out noticeably because what
follows is more of Jacob's instruction to and conversation with Enos,
but none of this is directly quoted. Why, then, does Jacob highlight
this succinct quotation?

To skip to the end of my analysis of this passage, I propose that
Jacob's direct quotation is part of putting Enos under covenant to care
for and continue the record. But first a few more details will help provide the context for this conclusion. Jacob was born while the family
wandered, the "first born . . . in the wilderness" (2 Nephi 2:1). When
Lehi, the family patriarch, blesses Jacob, he says, "Thy days shall be
spent in the service of thy God"; the phrase "in the service" specifically
indicated temple service in the Hebrew Bible (2 Nephi 2:3). Fast forward a few chapters to after Lehi's death when Nephi and his people are
developing their fledgling nation—planting crops, raising flocks, forg-
ing weapons, building buildings (2 Nephi 5:11–15). They build a temple
too, and ten verses later Nephi records that he "did consecrate Jacob
and Joseph, that they should be priests and teachers" (2 Nephi 5:26).
In this same chapter Nephi identifies himself as a *ruler* and teacher to
the people (v. 19), but Jacob is a *priest* and teacher who, according to
Lehi's instruction, will spend his days in the service of his God. Jacob,
the firstborn outside the purview of the temple at Jerusalem, is made a
priest of the Nephite temple and caretaker of the sacred Nephite records
on the small plates.[6] When we see that Jacob administers covenants in

---

5. I have used Royal Skousen's *The Book of Mormon: The Earliest Text* (New Haven:
Yale University Press, 2009) for Book of Mormon quotations.

6. Joseph Fielding Smith stated that those ordained to the Melchizedek Priesthood, such as Jacob and Joseph, carried out Levitical responsibilities with the Melchizedek Priesthood. Under the Mosaic law such responsibilities presumably would have
included administering animal sacrifices at the temple. See Joseph Fielding Smith,
Answers to Gospel Questions (Salt Lake City: Deseret Book, 1957), 1:124–25. Huldah's
reform in 2 Kings 22–23 demonstrates that the Israelites kept their sacred records in the
temple and that it was the responsibility of the temple priests to preserve those writings
and to make sure that the people were abiding by their precepts. See Julie M. Smith,

the temple, we can better appreciate how completely his relationship to covenants suffuses his leadership and his writings.

Covenant obligation to scripture

When Jacob says to Enos, "Take these plates," he invokes the covenant responsibility that attends to caring for and keeping the record. The placement of this injunction and its status as a direct quotation calls our attention to it, and within this unexpected passage the word *take* jumps out in particular: it is the most obvious imperative statement we have from Jacob in the chapter, and it recalls at least one poignant connection found earlier in his record between the word *take* and Jacob's covenantal responsibilities as temple priest. Jacob introduces his record by writing, "I, Jacob, *take* it upon me to fulfill the commandment of my brother Nephi" (Jacob 1:8), meaning to care for the plates and keep the record. Later in that opening chapter he writes,

> We did magnify our office unto the Lord, *taking* upon us the responsibility, answering the sins of the people upon our own heads if we did not teach them the word of God with all diligence; wherefore by laboring with our mights, their blood might not come upon our garments; otherwise their blood would come upon our garments and we would not be found spotless at the last day. (Jacob 1:19)

In these two examples, Jacob takes it upon himself to fulfill Nephi's commandment to keep the plates and keep the record, and he *takes* responsibility for the sins of his people in magnifying his office—his temple office—that in teaching his people the scriptures, their blood may not come upon his garments. Jacob's language of taking the people's blood on his own garments clearly connects his responsibility to teach—including teaching scripture or the "word of God"—with temple sacrifice and sprinkling of blood rituals. Thus, Jacob's use of

---

"Huldah's Long Shadow," in *A Dream, a Rock, and a Pillar of Fire: Reading 1 Nephi 1*, ed. Adam S. Miller (Provo, UT: Neal A. Maxwell Institute, 2017), 1–16.

the word *take* connects his responsibility to care for the plates with making covenants.

Jacob's linking of the word *take* to the practice of covenants is unusual. Nephi employs more common uses of the word, such as Zoram taking courage, the brothers taking the daughters of Ishmael to wife, the family taking their tents, or Laman and Lemuel seeking to take Nephi's life. But Jacob's use of the word is more precise.[7] One passage from Isaiah illustrates Jacob's pointed use of the word as compared to Nephi's more common usage. Both Nephi and Jacob quote Isaiah 49, but when Jacob comes to the word *take*, he inserts his own commentary after "even the captives of the mighty shall be taken away, and the prey of the terrible shall be delivered" (1 Nephi 21:25; 2 Nephi 6:17). To this Jacob adds, "For the mighty God shall deliver his covenant people." When he preached this verse, Jacob associated the word *take* with God's delivering his covenant people.

So when Jacob hands over the record to Enos and says, "Take these plates," in the context of Jacob's writings, these words have a covenant resonance. Jacob transfers more than plates; he binds Enos in a distinctly covenantal responsibility to care for and keep the plates. This covenant also includes an understanding that at some point in the future the record will one day save the descendants of their family.[8] Enos understands it as such when in his own account he describes, "I did cry unto God that he would preserve the records. And he covenanted with me that he would bring them forth unto the Lamanites in his own due time" (Enos 1:16). Enos asked for and received for himself confirmation of God's covenant to bless and reach his family through the plates. As we will see, this reiteration of covenants of gathering and family shows itself in Jacob's writing as well.

How do the small plates—or, for the purposes of this essay, how does scripture—save the family? Jacob's telling of his interaction with Sherem provides some insights. With this background of Jacob's view of the responsibility to the plates as a covenant obligation, and

---

7. See 1 Nephi 4:35; 7:1; 16:12; 2 Nephi 5:2.

8. Nephi sees the fate of his descendants and the descendants of Laman and Lemuel in his vision in 1 Nephi 12–13. See 1 Nephi 13:35–41 in particular.

remembering his immersion in and administration of covenants as the temple priest, we can recognize that Jacob also records the story of Sherem using language and imagery resonant of temple sacrificial covenants. Understanding that Jacob links his temple service to his covenantal responsibility to scripture and its consequent power to save his posterity, we see that the portrayal of the Sherem story has covenant implications for scripture and its power to save and reclaim families.

Jacob and Sherem's interaction as temple sacrifice

The confrontation between Jacob and Sherem may have had serious implications under the Mosaic law. Sherem brings what could be a formal accusation against Jacob saying,

> Brother Jacob, . . . ye have led away much of this people, that they pervert the right way of God and keep not the law of Moses, which is the right way, and convert the law of Moses into the worship of a being which ye say shall come many hundred years hence. And now behold, I Sherem declare unto you that this is blasphemy. (Jacob 7:6–7)

Sherem accuses Jacob of blasphemy and not keeping the Mosaic law. John Welch suggests that if Sherem indeed saw Jacob's teachings as desecrating the law of Moses, Sherem "would have had a legal or moral duty . . . to either take legal action against Jacob or risk falling under the wrath and judgment of God."[9] If Jacob were found guilty of such allegations, he would certainly be removed from his place as the leading priest in the Nephite temple and, under some readings of the Mosaic law, could potentially be stoned to death.[10] Clearly there is much more at stake than a garden-variety theological disagreement. If Jacob, the temple priest and guardian of the plates, could be denounced or found

---

9. John W. Welch, "The Case of Sherem," in *The Legal Cases in the Book of Mormon* (Provo, UT: BYU Press and Neal A. Maxwell Institute, 2008), 111.

10. Identifying Jacob as the "leading priest" is Welch's phrase. See Welch, "Case of Sherem," 115, and also Leviticus 24:10–16.

guilty, the entire tenor and trajectory of Nephite teachings of messianism would probably change as well.[11]

Sherem's accusation carries high stakes for Jacob's role as the head priest and for the Nephite religion regarding the doctrine of Christ, and the location of the confrontation itself may have similarly heightened the impact and import of this encounter between Jacob and Sherem. Welch raises the possibility that Sherem confronted Jacob in the temple courtyard itself, symbolically as well as verbally positioning himself against Jacob's priestly role and teachings.[12] Supposing that Jacob and Sherem did meet at or near the temple helps make sense of their interaction that follows.

Jacob describes their interaction, which may have occurred at the temple, as a kind of temple sacrifice. After describing Sherem's accusation and argument, Jacob explains, "the Lord God poured in his Spirit into my soul" (Jacob 7:8). The repetition of the direction—"in" and "into"—calls attention to this passage where even one use of the word "in" makes the phrase unique in scripture. The Latter-day Saint English edition of the standard works refers nearly thirty times to the Lord pouring his spirit. While acknowledging the impossibility of translating prepositions consistently across languages and ages, this passage in Jacob 7:8 is the only instance of the Lord pouring *in* his spirit.[13] In all other cases, the spirit is poured *out* or *on*, and almost always poured out over a people or a group. Consider the day of Pentecost and Peter's citation of Joel prophesying, "I will pour out of my Spirit upon all flesh" (Acts 2:17; see Joel 2:28). Isaiah quotes the Lord as saying, "I will pour

---

11. Incidentally, Jacob is the first to use the name Christ in the Book of Mormon, and after mentioning it in 2 Nephi 10, Nephi and all subsequent Book of Mormon prophets take up the name with the frequency that the Book of Mormon is well known for.

12. Welch explains, "There are reasons to think that Sherem confronted Jacob in a public place like the city gate, temple courtyard, or a gathering place where such controversies were normally heard." Welch, "Case of Sherem," 116. He cites Ludwig Köhler's appendix, "Justice in the Gate," in *Hebrew Man: Lectures Delivered at the Invitation of the University of Tübingen, December 1–16, 1952*, trans. Peter R. Ackroyd (New York: Abingdon, 1956), 127–32.

13. I want to acknowledge the impossibility of translating prepositions consistently across all languages and ages, but with roughly thirty examples in the English edition of the standard works in LDS scripture, this passage stands out as unique.

my spirit upon thy seed" (Isaiah 44:3). Later in the Book of Mormon the Lord pours out "his Spirit upon the Lamanites" (Helaman 6:36). The Doctrine and Covenants promises the Lord's spirit will be poured out on the Saints "in the day that they assemble themselves together" (D&C 44:2). When we see how many times the Lord pours *out* his spirit on a group, the repetition of the prepositions *in* and *into* in Jacob 7:8 calls even greater attention to the filling, internal, personal quality of the spirit that Jacob claims, and it presents a greater contrast to the other passages of pouring the spirit. Generally, this pouring out seems diffuse and broad, evoking the imagery of the windows of heaven pouring out a blessing without room to receive it. But Jacob's assertion is that, in this instance, the site of reception is very exact. It is as though Jacob is a vessel the spirit can fill up, and in using this language Jacob echoes priestly anointing imagery.

When priests performed temple service in ancient times, they received anointing oil that was poured [*yatsaq* יצק (Leviticus 8:12)] into their cupped left hand. From there the priest would dip from the cupped hand to anoint the sacrifice, smearing [*mashach* משח (Leviticus 8:10)] it with the oil. After a life of familiarity with temple acts such as pouring oil and anointing sacrifices, when Jacob empha-sizes—in a phrase unique in scripture—that the Lord God poured in his Spirit *into* Jacob's soul, he may be describing how the Lord God poured his Spirit *into* Jacob, *yatsaq*. In a sacrificial offering, the *mashach* follows.

After the Spirit is poured in into Jacob's soul, he asks Sherem, "Deniest thou the Christ, which should come?" (Jacob 7:9). They debate, and Jacob appeals to what he has heard and seen and testifies, "It also hath been made manifest unto me by the power of the Holy Ghost— wherefore I know if there should be no atonement made, all mankind must be lost" (Jacob 7:12). If the pouring of the Spirit was the *yatsaq*, this testimony and appeal to the power of the Holy Ghost acts as the *mashach*, or anointing. The sacrifice and covenant follow.

In temple sacrifice an animal offering is smitten and killed on the altar. When Jacob asserts the necessity of the atonement, Sherem replies, "Show me a sign by this power of the Holy Ghost, in the which ye know so much" (Jacob 7:13). Jacob declares that if God smites

Sherem, "Let that be a sign unto thee that [God] has power both in heaven and in earth and also that Christ shall come," after which the "power of the Lord came upon him," so much so that he fell to the earth (Jacob 7:14, 15). As Jacob frames it, Sherem is anointed and smitten, just as a temple offering would have been.

But the oblique image of Sherem as a covenant sacrificial figure goes further still. Jacob also writes a sort of simile curse into the story. In ancient Israelite temple ceremonies, the sacrificed animal stood as a proxy for the covenant maker. As proxy, the sacrificial animal took on a simile curse, physically bearing the consequence of what would happen to the covenant maker if the covenant terms were not met.[14] Sherem comes to Jacob purportedly in the interest of the people, calling the doctrine of Christ a perversion of the law of Moses. Having "labored diligently" to preach to the people, Sherem comes as a kind of proxy for the people as he confronts Jacob, possibly on the steps of the Nephite temple (Jacob 7:3). Sherem is smitten by the "power of the Lord" and falls to the earth. At his confession the "power of God" comes down upon the people such that they fall to the earth, enacting Sherem's fate in their realization of the consequences of denying Christ in the law (Jacob 7:15, 21). By falling to the earth, the people identify with Sherem and illustrate how the encounter is cast as a covenant. They take Sherem's fate as their own simile curse in a ratification ceremony that symbolizes their promised obedience to God.[15]

But if the story of Sherem suggests a figurative covenant ritual, what is the covenant? If Sherem stands in for the people, how is the people's obedience to God renewed and reinvigorated? Jacob writes Sherem's story and its effect upon the people with covenant overtones and then moves on rather abruptly to conclude that, as a result, they "searched the scriptures" and that "many means were devised to reclaim and restore the Lamanites to the knowledge of the truth" (Jacob 7:23–24).

14. Ben Spackman, "What Is a Covenant?" *Mormon Monastery*, http://www.mormonmonastery.org/covenant/.

15. George E. Mendenhall and Gary A. Herion, "Covenant," in *Anchor Bible Dictionary*, ed. David Noel Freedman (New York: Doubleday, 1992), 1:1185.

Covenant obligation to scripture

I propose that the people's renewed interest in scripture and in reclaiming the Lamanites is not a scene change but a continuation of Jacob's emphasis on covenant renewal. Sherem alleges that he believes the scriptures, to which Jacob responds, "Then ye do not understand them, for they truly testify of Christ" (Jacob 7:11). In Sherem's confession, his greatest concern about lying to God stems from admitting that he denied the Christ while declaring that he believed the scriptures. He says, "I fear lest I have committed the unpardonable sin, for I have lied unto God. For I denied the Christ and said that I believed the scriptures" (Jacob 7:19). Sherem then attests that the scriptures truly testify of Christ. The implication for the people is clear: If they don't know how to find Christ in their observance of the law, they don't know the scriptures sufficiently well. Thus, the people's obligation is, first and foremost, to return to the scriptures.

This renewed interest in scripture, specifically by the people, rather than their political or ecclesiastical leaders, may be the beginning of the increased popular access to scripture evident later in the Book of Mormon. When the people fell to the earth, it pleased Jacob, who "had requested it of [his] Father which was in heaven" (Jacob 7:22). This request makes more sense if the people's falling to the earth is their ratification to learn from Sherem, to avoid his fate, and to return to the scriptures. Perhaps this event was a pivot between the more exclusive access to scripture seen in the small plates and the wider use of scripture in the large plates.

But the people's return to the scriptures following Sherem's death was only one part of a covenant obligation to scripture. Besides the people returning to scriptures themselves, we see a renewed interest in bringing the Lamanites to a knowledge of the truth. Directly after the verse that says the people "searched the scriptures" the account reads, "And it came to pass that many means were devised to reclaim and restore the Lamanites to the knowledge of the truth" (Jacob 7:23, 24). This renewed interest in the Lamanites followed Sherem's death as a typological figure of temple sacrifice. The covenant associated with the sacrifice coincides with the people's return to scripture, which

Jacob also feels as a covenant responsibility, and leads to their efforts to restore the truth to their brethren, the Lamanites, pointing to the covenants binding families.

This concern to reclaim the Lamanites is a particularly strong theme throughout the small plates. Jacob puts Enos under covenant to keep and care for the plates, and Enos seeks a covenant promise from God that God would "preserve a record" of the Nephites, "that it might be brought forth some future day unto the Lamanites, that perhaps they might be brought unto salvation" (Enos 1:13). Over and over in the Book of Mormon we find that God's covenant to preserve the record functions as a way of preserving the Lamanites so that eventually those words can bring Lamanite descendants back into a covenant relation with God (see 1 Nephi 13:30–39). The survival of the record marks this covenant and also becomes a token of it.

Reauthoring covenants

While the details of ancient Israelite temple rites may resonate with the story of Sherem, it is still disconcerting that Jacob would portray Sherem as a kind of sacrificial offering. We cannot know to what extent the story is a faithful historical account and to what extent Jacob portrays it as he does for another purpose. Joseph Spencer has argued that the Book of Mormon asks its readers to consider how Book of Mormon authors understood their stories in light of previous scripture, that is, how a typological view of scriptural accounts and events informs Book of Mormon prophets' understanding of their own experiences.[16] The implication is that we can find such typological correspondences to scripture in our own experiences as well. Nephi engages this kind of reading and calls it likening the scriptures to themselves, reimagining scripture in light of his perspective and lived experiences (see 1 Nephi 19:23). For example, Nephi uses the exodus as inspiration for

---

16. See Joseph Spencer, *An Other Testament: On Typology*, 2nd ed. (Provo, UT: Neal A. Maxwell Institute, 2016). While keeping in mind Barthes's critique of biographical criticism, the Book of Mormon provides, as Joseph Spencer has shown, an approach for how it is to be read by modeling how its authors read scripture and, as I am arguing here, how they rewrite scripture.

his family's journey and writes the account in exodus terms.[17] Or, as another example, he places his own visions and the prophecies of his family among the visions and prophecies of Isaiah.

In like manner, Jacob weaves his own experiences and teachings together with those of other scriptural accounts and types. Jacob ties Zenos's extensive olive tree allegory to prophecies regarding the latter days. He frames his interaction with Sherem such that it resonates with the Mosaic law sacrifice. Right out of the gate, the first two Book of Mormon authors rework their own stories in and through the lens of other scripture, likening it to themselves.

In the story of Sherem, however, Jacob does more than liken the scriptures to himself; he recasts a covenant, a combination of likening and rewriting that I am calling "reauthoring." By "reauthor" I do not mean that it is for Jacob or any other person to revise or reset the terms of a covenant offered by God since God is the author and finisher of faith (see Hebrews 12:2; Moroni 6:4). Rather, following Jacob's lead, to reauthor is to take a covenant (or scripture) into one's own life by rewriting one's life into the scripture. Jacob writes blood sacrifice into his experience with Sherem and writes his experience with Sherem into the narrative of the Nephites' relationship to scripture and to the Lamanites. In doing so he creates scripture as he broadens the reach of already-existing scripture.

Jacob's reauthoring not only contains echoes of other scriptural accounts but specifically addresses covenants, namely the covenants of scripture. Jacob's account shows the covenant obligation to preserve scripture (e.g., Jacob placing Enos under covenant to "take these plates"), it shows the need to turn to scripture to avoid Sherem's fate (e.g., the people's ratification of the simile curse), and it shows that our

---

17. For example, Nephi refers to the exodus and to the wandering of the children of Israel explicitly in 1 Nephi 17:23–33. For commentaries on recurring themes of the exodus in the Book of Mormon, see George S. Tate, "The Typology of the Exodus Pattern in the Book of Mormon," in *Literature of Belief: Sacred Scripture and Religious Experience*, ed. Neal E. Lambert (Provo, UT: BYU Religious Studies Center, 1981), 245–62; and S. Kent Brown, "The Exodus Pattern in the Book of Mormon," in *From Jerusalem to Zarahemla: Literary and Historical Studies of the Book of Mormon* (Provo, UT: BYU Religious Studies Center, 1998), 75–98.

engagement with scripture is tied to a broader concern with family (e.g., the people "searched the scriptures" and devised means "to reclaim and restore the Lamanites to the knowledge of the truth"). Jacob's account of the covenants of scripture, together with his son Enos's subsequent prayer (after being put under covenant to care for the scriptural record), shows scripture as fundamental to the covenants of family.

Through Jacob 7 we see a pattern emerge: When these early Book of Mormon authors considered their covenant obligation to scripture, they necessarily also encountered the covenants of God to their brethren, their descendants, and the house of Israel. In short, they encountered God's covenants to their family. But this relationship shows that the meaning of *family* pertains to a much larger family than immediate blood relatives. Ultimately, it encompasses peoples, cities, kingdoms, and civilizations. Family, exceeding the bounds of domestic life, includes those who have preceded us and those who will follow, stretching across the history of the world. It requires us to care about the salvation of strangers.[18]

As Jacob's people turned to the scriptures in a covenantal way, they turned to their brethren. In the centuries that follow, the Nephites and Lamanites rewrote their relationship with each other over and over. In the final chapter of his record, Jacob reauthors his interaction with Sherem as well as his passing of the plates to Enos in covenant terms. The two covenants in Jacob 7 are two halves of one whole, one covenant that pours together salvation of the family with our obligation to the scriptures.

The story of Jacob and Sherem shows us as readers of the Book of Mormon that we are saved by covenants that bind us to God and to one another, and we find our place in those covenants by relating our lived experience of covenants to the experiences of others in scripture. Through the lens of scripture we write covenants into our lives and thus reauthor our experiences of covenants saving us and our families.

---

18. This connection between scripture and family reminds us of the related etymology between *covenant* and *testament*. See Wouter Van Beek, "Covenant," in *Encyclopedia of Mormonism* (New York: Macmillan, 1992), 331–33.

Formed by Family: Jacob 7 as a Site for Sealing

Jenny Webb

Endings

AT THE END OF HIS WRITINGS, and near the end of his life as well, Jacob appears to be winding down, tying up loose threads. Sherem has died, and the Nephites have returned to searching the scriptures. They make various attempts to reclaim the Lamanites, but when these attempts fail, the Nephites fortify themselves and turn to God. There is a sense that, in these final verses, Jacob is simply skimming over the top of a potentially complex narrative in order to reach, at last, a place to stop and rest. In verse 27, the final verse, Jacob's words clearly indicate the end he sees approaching:

> And I Jacob saw that I must soon go down to my *grave*; wherefore I said unto my son Enos: *Take these plates.* And I told him the things which my brother Nephi had commanded me, and he promised obedience unto the commands. And *I make an end of my writing* upon these plates, which writing hath been small. And to the reader

> *I bid farewell*, hoping that many of my brethren may read
> my words. Brethren, *adieu*.[1] (Jacob 7:27)

Death, inheritance, an end to writing, farewell, and *adieu*—the verse could scarcely be any more thematically clearer: this is the end.

And yet, it's clearly *not* the end. While Jacob may die, his preaching in 2 Nephi 9 plainly indicates that Jacob did not see death as an absolute end; rather, all die, but all will be resurrected and continue as "living souls."[2] There is also an odd temporality at play in the phrases "take these plates" and "I make an end of my writing." In each case, the very existence of those words *within* the book of Jacob itself witnesses that those words were not, in fact, an end. Jacob may have passed the plates to Enos, but he still retained some sort of authoritative access to them, or else he would not have been able to write about the experience on the plates themselves. And the same sort of temporal torsion occurs as Jacob makes "an end of [his] writing": any time narrators tell an audience they are ending, they do so precisely through an act of *not* ending. Even Jacob's final "farewell" and "adieu" undermine the concept of a final ending. He bids farewell specifically to "the reader," but then in the same breath expresses his hope that the reading (and therefore, the hypothetical reader) will continue as his words are (potentially) read by his brethren. And that final, terminal *adieu* that has caused so many interpretive difficulties? It is a farewell, yes, but a farewell that specifically orients the audience to a future—a future with God.[3] Jacob may be wrapping things up, but he's doing so in ways that make clear his faith: his faith in the power of the atonement to redeem flesh, his faith that his words will continue to be read, and his faith that his nebulous brethren (Nephites? Lamanites? us?) will, at the end of all things, be with God.

---

1. I have used Royal Skousen's *The Book of Mormon: The Earliest Text* (New Haven: Yale University Press, 2009) as my base text for Book of Mormon quotations; any emphasis has been added.

2. See, for example, 2 Nephi 9:13: "And the spirit and the body is restored to itself again, and all men become incorruptible and immortal; and they are living souls."

3. From the French *à* meaning "to," and *Dieu* meaning "God."

What is it that has marked Jacob's psyche such that, even at the end of his life and work, his words betray his underlying hope for connection and continuation? We have a hint here in verse 27 itself: Jacob passes the plates to Enos, *his son,* instructing him the same way that Nephi, *his brother,* had done, and then orients his final hope toward *his brethren.* In other words, Jacob's life, work, and writings are indelibly marked by Jacob's identity within the structure of the family. Jacob 7 is haunted in unacknowledged ways by Jacob's own family. These family connections stretch Jacob's temporal perspective beyond the boundaries of birth, life, and death—for Jacob, his family remains present to him, sealed up, and he to them, through a mixture of text and covenant.

Lehi: A visionary man

By the time Jacob writes this final chapter, Jacob 7, he is old. His life has, in many ways, come to pass. And in its passing, this life has been marked by a series of losses: a father, a mother, a city he never knew, and his brothers. Even Nephi, who, at Lehi's direction, stepped in to care for Jacob, has, by the time we reach this chapter, gone the way of all flesh. A remnant from the quickly receding past, Jacob's own body witnesses the liminal space of pilgrimage: born in the wilderness, between the memory of Jerusalem and the hope of the promised land.

Consider Jacob's relationship with his father, Lehi. Before his death, Lehi gives Jacob a blessing in 2 Nephi 2:1–4.

> And now Jacob, I speak unto you: Thou art my first born in the days of my tribulation in the wilderness. And behold, in thy childhood thou hast suffered afflictions and much sorrow because of the rudeness of thy brethren.
>
> Nevertheless, Jacob my first born in the wilderness, thou knowest the greatness of God. And he shall consecrate thine afflictions for thy gain.
>
> Wherefore thy soul shall be blessed, and thou shalt dwell safely with thy brother Nephi, and thy days shall

be spent in the service of thy God. Wherefore I know that thou art redeemed because of the righteousness of thy Redeemer, for thou hast beheld that in the fullness of time he cometh to bring salvation unto men.

And thou hast beheld in thy youth his glory, wherefore thou art blessed even as they unto whom he shall minister in the flesh. For the Spirit is the same yesterday, today, and forever, and the way is prepared from the fall of man, and salvation is free.

In these verses, Lehi identifies Jacob with the title "first born in the wilderness." He then blesses Jacob that God will "consecrate [his] afflictions for [his] gain," places him in the care of his brother Nephi, and consecrates him to a life of temple service (his birthright as a firstborn). Lehi uses his knowledge of Jacob's own spiritual experiences regarding the Messiah in order to launch into a theological discussion on grace, redemption, sin, law, and, most significantly, the Messiah. Shortly after this blessing, Lehi dies.

But Lehi's death is clearly not the end of Lehi's influence upon Jacob's life. What happens when someone loses their father at a relatively young age? Where would Jacob have turned to find the witness and evidence of his father's life? How does one seek recompense for such loss?

Jacob seeks his father through Lehi's own words. It is no accident that in his initial introduction of himself, Jacob reveals both an underlying psychological structure (anxiety) and his response to that structure: "Yea, mine anxiety is great for you. And ye yourselves know that it ever has been, for I have exhorted you with all diligence. *And I have taught you the words of my father*, and I have spoken unto you concerning all things which are written from the creation of the world" (2 Nephi 6:3). Worried and wearied, Jacob seeks solace in the word. While we do not have access to Lehi's own writings, we know they were substantial. The combined weight of pressed text and absent flesh produced an indelible mark upon Jacob's own writing—Lehi's prophetic legacy haunts Jacob's own ministerial efforts.

The problem for us, of course, is that we do not have direct access to the majority of Lehi's words, and therefore creating any kind of actual textual link evidencing some sort of paternal/authorial influence by Lehi upon Jacob seems futile. But what we do have are Nephi's summaries and quotations of his father's experiences. If we turn to 1 Nephi 1, for example, and examine the points Nephi highlights, it is a reasonably safe assumption that Jacob would have read similar content in the original words of Lehi.

> 4 For it came to pass in the commencement of the first year of the reign of Zedekiah, king of Judah—my father Lehi having dwelt at Jerusalem in all his days—and in that same year there *came many prophets prophesying* unto the people that they must repent or *the great city Jerusalem must be destroyed.*
>
> 5 Wherefore it came to pass that my father Lehi, as he went forth, *prayed* unto the Lord, yea, even *with all his heart*, in behalf of his people.
>
> 6 And it came to pass as he prayed unto the Lord, there came a pillar of fire and dwelt upon a rock before him, and he *saw* and *heard* much. And because of the things which he *saw* and *heard*, he did *quake* and *tremble* exceedingly.
>
> 7 And it came to pass that he returned to his own house at Jerusalem. And he *cast* himself upon his bed, being *overcome* with the Spirit and the things which he had *seen*.
>
> 8 And being thus overcome with the Spirit, he was carried away in a *vision*, even that he saw the heavens open and he thought he saw God sitting upon his throne, surrounded with numberless concourses of angels in the attitude of singing and praising their God.
>
> 9 And it came to pass that he saw *one* descending out of the midst of heaven, and he beheld that his luster was above that of the sun at noonday.

10 And he also saw *twelve* others following him, and their brightness did exceed that of the stars in the firmament.

11 And they came down and went forth upon the face of the earth. And the first came and stood before my father and gave unto him a *book* and bade him that he should *read*.

12 And it came to pass that as he *read*, he was filled with the Spirit of the Lord.

13 And he read, saying: Woe woe unto Jerusalem, for I have seen thine abominations. Yea, and many things did my father read concerning Jerusalem, that it should be *destroyed* and the inhabitants thereof; many should perish by the sword and many should be carried away captive into Babylon. . . .

15 And after this manner was the language of my father in the *praising* of his God, for his soul did rejoice and his *whole heart was filled* because of the things which he had *seen*, yea, which the Lord had shewn unto him.

16 And now I Nephi do not make a full account of the things which my father hath written, for he hath written many things which he saw in *visions* and in *dreams*. And he also hath *written* many things which he *prophesied* and *spake* unto his children, of which I shall not make a full account. . . .

18 Therefore I would that ye should know that after the Lord had shewn so many marvelous things unto my father Lehi, yea, concerning the destruction of Jerusalem, behold, *he went forth* among the people and began to *prophesy* and to *declare* unto them concerning the things which he had both *seen* and *heard*.

19 *And it came to pass that the Jews did mock him because of the things which he testified of them, for he truly testified of their wickedness and their abomina- tions. And he testified that the things which he saw and heard, and also the things which he read in the book,*

manifested plainly of the coming of a Messiah and also the redemption of the world.

20 And when the Jews heard these things, they were *angry* with him, yea, even as with the *prophets* of old, whom they had *cast out* and stoned and slain. And they also sought his life that they might take it away. (1 Nephi 1:4–13, 15–16, 18–20)

Notice the initial emphasis on prophecy in verse 4, the connection between flesh and revelation in verse 6, and Lehi's choice to respond to his experiences both with praise and by then enacting the role of the prophet himself. Lehi's individual experiences here lay out a type of template for both prophetic experience and content:

1. Receives the prophecies of others
2. Turns to Lord, seeking in prayer
3. Receives his own vision (both seen and heard)
   a. Is overcome by that vision (i.e., has ready access to emotions)
4. Receives another vision
   a. God and angels
   b. Christ and apostles
   c. Book and coming destruction
5. Records his prophecies
6. Prophesies and declares to people
7. Witnesses
   a. Sin
   b. Messiah
8. Is rejected

The content of his prophecy in verse 19 is most telling: "And he testified that the things which he saw and heard, and also the things which he read in the book, manifested plainly of the *coming of a Messiah, and also the redemption of the world.*" The beating heart of Lehi's prophetic act lies in his utter commitment to the messianic. It is no surprise, then, that that same messianism flows throughout Jacob's own veins. It is this messianism against which Sherem complains, and to which Jacob replies in Jacob 7:11–12: "And I saith unto him: Then ye do not understand them [the scriptures], for they truly *testify of Christ*. Behold, I say unto you that none of the prophets have written nor prophesied save they have spoken concerning this *Christ*. And this is not all. It hath been made manifest unto me—for I have *heard* and *seen* and it also hath been made manifest unto me by the power of the Holy Ghost—wherefore, I know if there should be no atonement made, all mankind must be lost."

In addition to the various thematic resonances between prophecy, vision, leading away, and rejection, the text in Jacob 7 frames Sherem's complaint as centering on "the gospel" of "the doctrine of Christ," who is, like Lehi's Messiah, "a being which ye say shall come many hundred years hence" (Jacob 7:7). In other words, Jacob paints Sherem's main accusation as a repetition of the very thing against which the Jews of Jerusalem reacted so strongly when Lehi originally preached it: "the coming of a messiah" (1 Nephi 1:19).

> And it came to pass that he came unto me and on this wise did he speak unto me, saying: Brother Jacob, I have sought much opportunity that I might speak unto you, for I have heard and also know that thou goest about much, preaching that which ye call the gospel or the doctrine of Christ.
>
> And ye have led away much of this people, that they pervert the right way of God and keep not the law of Moses, which is the right way, and convert the law of Moses into the worship of a being which ye say shall come many hundred years hence. And now behold, I Sherem declare unto you that this is blasphemy, for no man knoweth of such things; for he cannot tell of things to come. And after this manner did Sherem contend against me. (Jacob 7:6–7)

The textual resonances here link Jacob's encounter with Sherem to Lehi's own words and experiences *as a prophet*. Jacob is not merely asserting some sort of lineal connection—the point is not so much that Lehi is Jacob's literal father, although that is significant in its own way. The point Jacob crafts as an author, rather, is to claim Lehi the prophet as his own progenitor: Lehi and Jacob share, in a fundamental sense, the same prophetic project of messianism.

At the same time, note how this address characterizes Jacob's prophetic experience as thematically familial, thus placing the prophetic within the realm of lineal (and thus enfleshed) inheritance:

- Sherem addresses him as "Brother Jacob," evoking theme of family (v. 6).
- Sherem characterizes Jacob's work as going about much "preaching," which directly echoes Lehi's pattern of prophecy (to go out and share the words) (v. 6).
- Sherem describes the effect of that preaching as having "led away much of this people," which is the result of Lehi's own preaching—the leading away of his own family and others into the wilderness (v. 7).
- Sherem centers his complaint around the rejection of the possibility of prophecy (v. 7).
- Sherem could be interpreted as "angry," just as the citizens of Jerusalem were angry with the prophets of old and with Lehi himself (v. 7).

In a certain sense, we can see in Jacob 7 Jacob's own subtle assertion of the fulfillment of the blessing his dying father pronounced on his head in 2 Nephi 2: Jacob claims his inheritance as Lehi's firstborn son in the wilderness. As such, Jacob inherits his father's prophetic pattern of receiving the word, preaching, and being rejected. Notice too how verses 5 and 7 of 1 Nephi 1 appear to indicate that Lehi's own initial vision took place outside Jerusalem, in a type of wilderness (the wilderness of being not at home)—in other words, Jacob's blessing as the firstborn in the wilderness was not merely geographically descriptive, but potentially spiritually descriptive. Jacob is the firstborn son who is born in the space where revelation and vision began for his father. Jacob 7 identifies Jacob as Lehi's firstborn son both in terms of thematic patterning (i.e., the prophetic motif) and in terms of theological content, with all the rights, privileges, and inheritances that identity implies, including the theological inheritance of an understanding of the coming Messiah as central to the law of Moses.

Nephi: Protector and king

Lehi isn't the only absent father figure for Jacob. Consider Jacob's relationship with his brother Nephi. At a relatively young age, Nephi becomes, for Jacob, the literal embodiment of the concept of family. How close were they? Lehi entrusts Jacob into Nephi's care, but how much care did Jacob then require? How often did Jacob depend upon Nephi for strength, for love, for protection, for teaching? How often did Jacob talk with Nephi about the scriptures? The Lamanites? His role as king? What did Jacob actually witness in Nephi as his brother? Did he see Nephi succeed? Did he see Nephi fail? We cannot, of course, find definite answers to these questions. But what we can find is clear evidence that Nephi's struggles resonated with Jacob.

Nephi tries so hard to hold himself together, to hold his family together. He gives us the story of his life, placing it within a narrative framework that, from the outside, exhibits an absolute confidence in the reality of God's hand. Perhaps in a community where Nephi occupies the role of king and protector, this narrative makes sense. However, this is not the narrative that Jacob brings out. Instead, he punctuates Jacob 7 with phrases that link Jacob's own experience with Sherem with Nephi's words in 2 Nephi 4 (and specifically the formalized emotion of Nephi's psalm).[4]

There are explicit thematic parallels between 2 Nephi 4 and Jacob 7. The confidence in prayer, the reception of visions and ministrations, and the language used to describe their trust in God produce thematic resonance, while the original pathos of 2 Nephi 4 reappears in Jacob 7

---

4. For additional work on Nephi's psalm and its poetic form as personal lament, see Steven P. Sondrup, "The Psalm of Nephi: A Lyric Reading," *BYU Studies* 21/3 (1981): 357–72; and Matthew Nickerson, "Nephi's Psalm: 2 Nephi 4:16–35 in the Light of Form-Critical Analysis," *Journal of Book of Mormon Studies* 6/2 (1997): 26–42.

as a mournful meditation on loss and wandering.[5] While these thematic parallels are enough to suggest the ongoing influence of Nephi upon Jacob's thoughts and work, there are specific textual connections that, when foregrounded, demonstrate the depth of the connection between the two brothers.

Table 1. Comparison of 2 Nephi 4 and Jacob 7

2 Nephi 4	Jacob 7
After Lehi "had spake unto all," he passes away (v. 12)	Sherem dies after "he had said these words" (v. 20)
Laman and Lemuel are angry with Nephi specifically over things Nephi has shared that have come "of the Lord" (v. 13)	Sherem complains against "the doctrine of Christ" (v. 6)
"I will not put my trust in the arm of flesh, for I know that cursed is he that putteth his trust in the arm of flesh. Yea, cursed is he that putteth his trust in man or maketh flesh his arm" (v. 34)	The Lamanites "sought by the power of their arms" to destroy the Nephites, who "did fortify against them with their arms" (vv. 24–25)
God "hath confounded mine enemies, unto the causing of them to quake before me" (v. 22)	"I did confound him in all his words" (v. 8)
"Yea, I know that God will give liberally to him that asketh; yea, my God will give me if I ask not amiss" (v. 35)	"I had requested it of my Father which was in heaven, for he had heard my cry and answered my prayer" (v. 22)
"He hath given me knowledge by visions in the nighttime. . . . Angels came down and ministered unto me" (vv. 23–24)	"I truly had seen angels and they had ministered unto me" (v. 5)
"I have seen so great things" (v. 26)	"For I have heard and seen" (v. 12)

(table continues)

---

5. See Jacob 7:26: "Wherefore I conclude this record, declaring that I have written according to the best of my knowledge, by saying that the time passed away with us, and also our lives passed away like as it were unto us a dream, we being a lonesome and a solemn people, wanderers cast out from Jerusalem, born in tribulation in a wild wilderness, and hated of our brethren, which caused wars and contentions; wherefore we did mourn out our days."

"My soul will rejoice in thee, my God and the rock of my salvation" (v. 30), and "I will cry unto thee, my God, the rock of my righteousness. Behold, my voice shall forever ascend up unto thee, my rock and mine everlasting God" (v. 35)	The Nephites are "trusting in the God and the rock of their salvation" (v. 25)

The connections between the two texts, while not overt upon a cursory reading, are more obvious when set side by side. Jacob's own textual formulations echo Nephi's words and experiences. Jacob is not simply framing his experiences in terms that are reminiscent of his brother's work: Jacob's own language, the phrasing and terminology he draws on as an author, is haunted by Nephi's words. Nephi is indelibly imprinted upon Jacob's linguistic soul.

Looking at the connections in 2 Nephi 4 as a whole (and not limiting ourselves to the psalm section), it is significant to note that the psalm emerges out of an experience Nephi has with Laman and Lemuel in which they become angry with Nephi because of words he has shared with them in his role as prophet. Laman and Lemuel do not want to hear the word of the Lord via their younger brother, just as Sherem does not want to hear Jacob preaching the doctrine of Christ. In each case, the overriding form is that of the rejection of a prophet (in other words, a part of the prophetic pattern established by their father, Lehi).

Are both Nephi and Jacob simply repeating the patterns of their father? When they use the same words and phrases while composing a text in order to process an act of rejection, are Nephi and Jacob reflecting the shared vocabulary of brothers who have lived and worked and talked together throughout their lives? Or are they passing down to us not only the life of their father but the textual effects of his preaching itself? Are we hearing Lehi's voice echo through his sons? However we decide to interpret these structural, thematic, and textual connections, it is clear that familial bonds are powerful and influential here. These bonds make Jacob's apparent solitude at the end of his life even more striking.

Laman and Lemuel: Brothers in conflict

Nephi is not the only brother whose relationship makes its mark in Jacob 7. Consider Jacob's relationship to his oldest brothers, Laman and Lemuel. Like Lehi, and like Nephi, Laman and Lemuel are gone by the time Jacob writes chapter 7. But, unlike Lehi and Nephi, Laman and Lemuel were, in a certain sense, gone before Jacob even arrived. It is not just Jacob but the entire family who are haunted by the continually present absence of Laman, Lemuel, and their families. The division here is fundamental to the entire project of the Book of Mormon itself: without this originary rift in the familial fabric, we would discuss the history of the Lehites, rather than the Nephites and Lamanites.

Jacob is born into a preexisting conflict—an open, weeping wound. The conflict here is explicitly religious: Laman and Lemuel's expectations of their lived religion emphasize notions of inheritance as codified under Mosaic law. To live right with the law is to live within a legal structure that identifies their worth through their birthright as elder brothers. However, as they attempt to follow the law and honor their father, their inheritance is repeatedly stripped away. They leave behind their possessions in Jerusalem, and then they lose them again to Laban. On the ship crossing the sea, Nephi, the younger brother, is clearly designated as the leader of the expedition, and then, in the promised land, Nephi and his people leave, taking the brass plates.[6] The issue here stems not just from a desire for political or economic power, but from a fundamentally conflicted understanding of what their religion was and how it was to be lived. To promise the Messiah is to promote a lived religion in which the force of the law has been, in a sense, emptied.[7] If the law is kept for the sake of a promised Messiah

---

6. Mosiah 10:11–17 makes it clear that the Lamanites considered this action robbery: "And again, they were wroth with him because he departed into the wilderness as the Lord had commanded him and took the records which were engraven on the plates of brass, for they said that he robbed them" (v. 16).

7. For example, see 2 Nephi 25:25: "For for this end was the law given. Wherefore the law hath become dead unto us, and we are made alive in Christ because of our faith, yet we keep the law because of the commandments."

and not for the sake of the law, then lawful inheritance is problematized in ways that Laman and Lemuel fail to grasp.

Put another way, Laman and Lemuel have use for the law as the means through which they can satisfy their desire for narrative control. Lehi, Nephi, and Jacob have faith in the coming Messiah. Laman and Lemuel consistently reject things that they cannot anticipate: they follow Lehi out of obedience to the law rather than faith in their father's visions; they do not believe they will get the brass plates; they do not think that Nephi can build a ship, and so forth. When Laman and Lemuel reach the promised land, they want to replicate the society from which they came: they want to live the law in order to receive their expected inheritance. But Nephi and Jacob are constantly preaching faith in a Christ they have not yet seen—and this tension literally cuts the family in two.

Notice the underlying reliance upon the law as law that Laman and Lemuel exhibit at the final breaking point in 2 Nephi 5:2–4:

> But behold, their anger did increase against me, insomuch that they did seek to take away my life. Yea, they did murmur against me, saying: Our younger brother thinketh to rule over us, and we have had much trial because of him. Wherefore now let us slay him, that we may not be afflicted more because of his words. For behold, we will not that he shall be our ruler, *for it belongeth unto us which are the elder brethren to rule over this people.* Now I do not write upon these plates all the words which they murmured against me, but it sufficeth me to say that they did seek to take away my life.

Unable to live in a situation they perceive as being outside the boundaries prescribed by law, Laman and Lemuel determine that the only thing they can do is remove the usurper, thus ending both his life and his voice. It is significant that the main source of affliction for Laman and Lemuel is not some form of political oppression or physical aggression on the part of Nephi, but rather "his words." Why would Nephi's words drive them to murder? Precisely because they are words that preach the coming Messiah and thus undo the law, shifting its power from force to grace.

When Jacob reacts to Sherem's accusations, he is also reacting to what Sherem represents: the potential for continued conflict and division within Jacob's extended sense of family (i.e., within his people). We might not like the strong element of damnation in Jacob's use of the phrases "thou art of the devil" and "wicked man" in verses 14 and 23, but we can certainly understand the continually present pain in Jacob's life that might motivate it. As a child, Jacob was entrusted to Nephi by his father precisely because his father could not count on Laman and Lemuel to prioritize familial bonds above the code of the law. The schism began before Jacob's birth, at the moment the family left Jerusalem and entered into a wilderness governed by revelation. It is quite possible that Jacob never had a chance at a brotherly relationship with Laman and Lemuel—they may have hated him from birth simply because, as a small child, he was more closely aligned with Lehi or because perhaps Nephi developed a relationship with him. In a very real sense, Jacob's brothers were lost to him before his birth such that his life was inevitably marked by a sense of sorrowful loss.

Articulating the ways in which family loss has been foundational for Jacob from the beginning helps us to see why, after Sherem's death, Jacob casts himself again into the project of reclamation and restoration: "And it came to pass that many means were devised *to reclaim and restore the Lamanites* to the knowledge of the truth; but it all were vain, for they delighted in wars and bloodsheds, and they had an eternal hatred against us their brethren, and they sought by the power of their arms to destroy us continually" (Jacob 7:24). Sealing this breach is a way to bind up his family. And the fact that Jacob continually works at this problem, constantly reaching out, trying new ideas, seeking connection, demonstrates his absolute belief and hope that the family is salvable.[8] In the context of Jacob 7, it is telling that, after so

---

8. We can see a parallel here then between Jacob's theology of flesh, especially as developed in 2 Nephi 9, and his theology of family: both are corruptible and prone to dissolution, but at the same time, both can be saved in and through the sealing power of the atonement of Christ. Through the atonement, broken bodies and spirits are reunited; through the atonement, fragmented families are gathered up and bound.

many losses, the one that Jacob actively pursues in the text rather than echoing through thematic and linguistic correspondence is this one: the fracture that was already set before his birth.

But Jacob's projects of reclamation do not succeed. "Wherefore, the people of Nephi did fortify against them with their arms and with all their might, trusting in the God and the rock of their salvation; wherefore, they became as yet conquerors of their enemies" (Jacob 7:25). The Lamanites continue to wage war, and the Nephites respond in like manner—the family remains broken. Is Jacob 7 solely a record of loss? Why create a text fundamentally informed by family in so many ways if only to tell us that, in the end, the family fails?

Enos: Future promise

Jacob's family does not end with his brothers. At the beginning of this investigation into the family relationships that haunt Jacob 7, we noted Jacob's emphasis on endings and farewell in verse 27. Returning to that verse now, we can see that Jacob also enacts a sort of family reunion in that same verse.

> And I Jacob saw that I must soon go down to my grave; wherefore I said unto my *son* Enos: Take these plates. And I told him the things which my *brother* Nephi had commanded me, and he promised obedience unto the commands. And I make an end of my writing upon these plates, which writing hath been small. And to the reader I bid farewell, hoping that many of my *brethren* may read my words. *Brethren*, adieu. (Jacob 7:27)

With Lehi's visions, expulsion, and pilgrimage in the background, Jacob finishes his writings by bringing together every faction in his fractured family: Nephi, the nebulous "brethren," who could be either Nephites or Lamanites, or even both—but leading them all we have the sudden appearance of a son. A son whose existence implies at the least a wife, if not other children, who, by this point in Jacob's life, would be grown with families of their own. After an entire chapter structured textually and thematically by a family whose primary mode is that of absence, we find Jacob in the thick of it here—embedded within the swirling mass of family bonds that pull him inexorably into the future just as much as they push him into the present and the past.

This family reunion, like all family reunions, is not about a stagnant, well-defined, finished family. It is instead about the family as an ongoing project that exists not in the present, not in the past, and not in the future, but instead in the thick soup of an extending (and distending) temporality. The family patterns thus repeat: Enos has read Jacob just as Jacob has read Lehi. "Behold, it came to pass that I Enos *knowing my father* that he was a just man, for he taught me in his language and also in the nurture and admonition of the Lord—and blessed be the name of my God for it" (Enos 1:1). Notice how the very first thing we learn about Enos, after his name, is his identity as a son, and specifically a son who *knew* his father, not only as a person, but as a prophet with all the patterns, themes, and motifs that word implies in this familial context.

On the surface, these two narratives could not appear more different: Jacob is confronted by another person, an enemy. They talk, and the enemy dies confessing Christ, witnessed by a textually nebulous "everyone." Enos, on the other hand, leaves "everyone" behind, goes into the wilderness to kill animals, and speaks not with an enemy but rather God. And the result is a covenant of life, not for Enos, or even his people, but for a text.

But Enos makes it clear that Jacob is very present on this particular hunting trip. When Enos finds himself with some time, he chooses to reflect on "the words which I had often heard my father speak concerning eternal life and the joy of the saints" (Enos 1:3). Reflecting on the words of one's father is something that this family does quite well, it appears; perhaps it's even some sort of tradition by this point. But the appearance of "joy" here is somewhat unexpected. Joy? Really? Jacob? It is quite possible that the inner authorial personality we find within the words of Jacob in 2 Nephi and Jacob does not correspond to the interactions his own family experienced. For all of Jacob's (potentially private) sadness, the message his *son* received is one centered around joy.

There are indications in the text that Enos had not only listened to the words his father spoke but also read the words his father wrote. For example, when Enos finds God, he explains that he knows "that God could not lie; wherefore [his] guilt was swept away" (Enos 1:6). There is an odd inversion here of Sherem's actual experience: Sherem fears that he has lied to God and then collapses, swept away by guilt, while Enos in turn finds joy in God's truthfulness such that he lets go of his guilt. The guilt, rather than Enos himself, is the object in motion in Enos's conversion narrative here as opposed to Sherem's experience of physical collapse. Enos himself stays rooted, planted in Christ, as if he experiences the conversion experience Sherem could have had, but didn't. And when Enos, in a beautiful moment, actually engages with God in response rather than turning away from God in relief, God responds with words that in every way sound as if they come from Jacob himself: "Because of thy faith in *Christ*, whom thou hast not *heard nor seen—* and many years *passeth away* before he shall manifest himself *in the flesh*—wherefore go to it; thy faith hath made thee whole" (Enos 1:8).

More textual connections with Jacob's words follow throughout the chapter: Enos's response is that his faith "began to be *unshaken*" (Enos 1:11),[9] and he recounts the futility of the struggles to restore the Lamanites to the truth (Enos 1:14). Enos's response to this witness in the wilderness is that he, like his fathers before him, "went about among the people of Nephi, *prophesying of things to come* and testifying of the things which [he] had *heard* and *seen*" (Enos 1:19). This description is a literal echo of 1 Nephi 1:18, in which Lehi "*went forth* among the people and began to *prophesy* and to *declare* unto them concerning the things which he had both *seen* and *heard*," and, of course, of Jacob's own experience as related in Jacob 7:11–12: "Behold, I say unto you that none of the prophets have written nor prophesied save they have spoken concerning this *Christ*. . . . It hath been made manifest unto me—for I have *heard* and *seen* and it also hath been made manifest unto me by the power of the Holy Ghost—wherefore

---

9. Echoing Jacob's description in 2 Nephi 9:40: "I know that the words of truth are hard against all uncleanness, but the righteous fear it not, for they love the truth and are not *shaken*."

I know if there should be no atonement made, all mankind must be lost." These textual traces echo a familial heritage of revelation and witnessing, linking Enos with his father, but also integrating him into a prophetic inheritance centered around the procurement, production, and protection of sacred texts *so that* a broken family may, one day, be bound up and healed.

The textual traces of Jacob's life grace the writings of Enos, standing as evidence of the sealing gesture enacted generationally. Jacob turns toward Enos in Jacob 7 in a way that interrupts the temporal narrative of the text: Jacob sees his impending death, and in response, points to life. Enos, in turn, reflects that sealing in his own turn toward his father at the beginning of his words. For Jacob, this "turning toward" enacted in his own familial relationships is one founded on hope. In the context of Mormon theology, this "turning toward" is central. For example, notice how Malachi 4:5–6[10] is given to the Nephites by Christ in 3 Nephi 25:5–6 and to Joseph Smith by the angel Moroni in Joseph Smith—History 1:38–39. Jacob's own focus on ancestors and descendants is not a singular, solitary event, but rather an essential pattern of the gospel plan. The underlying hope in this generational turning is not just the hope for a single family, but hope that the human family can and will turn together, sealing past, present, and future into the family known in doctrinal terms as the house of Israel. Jacob's gesture here at the end of Jacob 7 produces a specific kind of hope: a hope for a salvation in Christ that raises flesh and redeems *families.* Jacob makes this final hope explicit at the end of verse 27: "And to the reader I bid farewell, *hoping* that many of my brethren may read my words." He ends on a sealing hope, a hope oriented toward the past as much as it is toward the future, a hope that, in the present moment of his writing, cannot contain its own excess.

The excess that Jacob cannot contain is the excess of flesh itself: the fleshiness of bodies exhibits a materiality that, in the context of the atonement, will be (and thus in a sense already is) raised from

---

10. "Behold, I will send you Elijah the prophet before the coming of the great and dreadful day of the Lord: And he shall turn the heart of the fathers to the children, and the heart of the children to their fathers, lest I come and smite the earth with a curse."

corruption to incorruption. Flesh reveals the truth of the family line: relationships are both fleshy and familial, temporal and eternal, metonymic and metaphoric,[11] individual and historical, visible and invisible.[12] Our bodies, in the very facticity of their conception, generation, and existence, serve as a site of revelation precisely in how they manifest the truth of our relationships. We come not just from some*where*, but from some*one*. We are bound not just through the sticky connectivity of generational flesh, but through time and eternity. Jacob's words fold in an act of bifurcating haunting: they are touched by the words of his father while simultaneously touching those of his son. Jacob shows us the family itself as a mode of prophecy: familial flesh witnesses Christ in the certainty of redemption. We are not raised from the dead simply to exist. We resurrect to live *together*.

---

11. My allusion to Lacan's terminology in "metonymic" and "metaphoric" is deliberate. If we begin at the site of the body, then the metonymic chain of combination leads from body to body, that is, to the family as generations. However, we can also begin at the body and trace the path of metaphor, which functions through substitution and symbol. The overlapping symbols thus generated produce meaning through condensation. And what is condensation but the revelation of a symbol's inherent valence? In other words, the metaphoric is analogous to the prophetic: each collapses or condenses signification such that temporal markers (past/present/future) are emptied out. Thus, from the body itself, the family enters two modalities: generation and prophecy. See Jacques Lacan, "The Instance of the Letter in the Unconscious, or Reason since Freud," in *Jacques Lacan, Écrits: The First Complete Edition in English*, trans. Bruce Fink (New York: W. W. Norton, 2006), 412–41.

12. It is useful here to recall the phenomenological account of flesh and bodies in the work of Maurice Merleau-Ponty. Flesh is polyvalent, both sensing and sensate, and this inherent relationality at the heart of flesh produces pliability. Pliable, flesh can feel and be felt: flesh folds, and a gap between the sensing and the sensible is held open in the experience of touch (Merleau-Ponty calls this gap *écart*). This phenomenological structuring of flesh helps to conceptualize what is at work in the act of sealing itself. Heaven and earth, in a sense, collapse together in the form of the fold, touching and touched together, but the gap, the necessary separation between the two, remains in place. Family relationships are inscribed along similar tensions, each of which can be "quilted" together to generate meaning. In practical terms, what I am advocating here is a dual understanding of Jacob in his family context and Jacob in the prophetic context, both of which only function through a mutually reversible relationality. See Maurice Merleau-Ponty, *The Visible and the Invisible*, ed. Claude Lefort, trans. Alphonso Lingis (Evanston: Northwestern University Press, 1968).

Jacob 7 clears a space by giving us his father through absence and his brother Nephi through absence, all while hoping to heal the predicative absence of his brethren. The Lamanites are absent, but they are not the absent Lamanites—to write them thus would be to deny the power of the Messiah to raise crumbling flesh and tie broken bonds in the flesh, through his flesh. Just as flesh crosses the cut between heaven and earth, the power of the risen flesh brings recompense through sealing. It is this hope (this joy) that Jacob passes on to his son Enos.

Jacob 7 serves as a site for this sealing. Throughout the chapter, Jacob stakes his claim: he is Lehi's son, Nephi's brother, Laman and Lemuel's brother despite rejection, and Enos's father. The presence (and absence) of these familial voices haunts Jacob 7, seeping up through its language, its composition, and its thematic structures. It serves as a text in which, in a very real way, a family is sealed together. In sealing, noncontinuous temporalities are bound together. Sealing frees up our temporal expectations of continuity through a cut that simultaneously delineates generational difference while covering over the division of that difference. In other words, sealing cuts off our relationship to sin through a turning of hearts that witnesses sin itself as a kind of gift, the kind of gift that re-turns us to ourselves again and again. When we repent, we open up a space for sealing flesh—we return to being penitent, humble, meek, and pliant. The plan is not what we think it is. The plan is not to seal *in*, it is to seal *up*—a familial redemption of rising flesh. As Latter-day Saints, we read Jacob and see him turn his heart in hope to the future, to our future, now. So we read, again and again, fleshy fingers tracing text and folding families into one.

Contributors

KIMBERLY M. BERKEY is a graduate student in philosophy of religion at Harvard Divinity School. Prior to graduate work, she studied as a Hinckley Scholar at Brigham Young University. She is the author of several articles on the Book of Mormon, including publications through the *Journal of Book of Mormon Studies.*

SHARON J. HARRIS is a PhD candidate in early modern English literature at Fordham University. Her research focuses on literary representations of music, and she is published in the *Ben Jonson Journal, Notes & Queries,* and the *Mormon Studies Review.* In Mormon studies, Sharon has been a participant in the summer seminar at the Neal A. Maxwell Institute for Religious Scholarship, the Mormon Theology Seminar, and the Wheatley Institute summer seminar. She holds degrees from Brigham Young University and the University of Chicago.

ADAM S. MILLER is a professor of philosophy at Collin College in McKinney, Texas. He earned a PhD in philosophy from Villanova University. He is the author of six books, including *Letters to a Young Mormon* (Neal A. Maxwell Institute, 2014), *The Gospel according to David Foster Wallace* (Bloomsbury, 2016), and *Future Mormon* (Greg Kofford Books, forthcoming). He directs the Mormon Theology Seminar and coedits a series of books for the Maxwell Institute entitled Groundwork: Studies in Theory and Scripture.

JACOB RENNAKER has a PhD in religious studies from Claremont Graduate University and has published articles on the Bible, Mesopotamian religion, Mormon scripture, and religion in popular culture. He also received degrees in comparative religion from the University of Washington and ancient Near Eastern studies from Brigham Young University. After wandering for years, he finally married the girl of his dreams and lives with her in California as Scholar in Residence and Director for the John A. Widtsoe Foundation.

JANA RIESS is a senior columnist for Religion News Service and holds a PhD in American religious history from Columbia University. She is the author or coauthor of numerous books, including *Flunking Sainthood, The Twible, Mormonism and American Politics*, and *Selections from the Book of Mormon, Annotated and Explained*.

JOSEPH M. SPENCER earned his PhD from the University of New Mexico and is currently visiting assistant professor in the Department of Ancient Scripture at Brigham Young University. He is the author of *For Zion* (Greg Kofford Books, 2014), *An Other Testament* (Neal A. Maxwell Institute, 2016), and most recently *The Vision of All: Twenty-Five Lectures on Isaiah in Nephi's Record* (Greg Kofford Books, 2016). He serves as the associate director of the Mormon Theology Seminar and is the editor of the *Journal of Book of Mormon Studies*. He and Karen, his wife, live in Provo, Utah, with their five children.

JEREMY WALKER lives in Utah and works for the Joseph Smith Papers as an editor. He did undergraduate work at Brigham Young University and graduate work at both the University of Colorado at Boulder and Brown University, where he studied literature and philosophy.

JENNY WEBB lives in Woodinville, Washington, with her husband, Nick Webb, and two children. She has an MA in comparative literature from Brigham Young University and works as an editor and production manager for several academic journals. She has contributed chapters to *Perspectives on Mormon Theology: Scriptural Theology; An Experiment on the Word: Reading Alma 32*; and *Reading Nephi*

Reading Isaiah: Reading 2 Nephi 26–27, which she coedited along with Joseph M. Spencer. She is the current president of Mormon Scholars in the Humanities and serves on the Mormon Theology Seminar executive board.